CAUGHT UP INTO PARADISE

Dr. Richard E. Eby

A true account of the experiences
of a boy and his family whom God
patiently and painfully guided
around, over, or through the human
problems of life on earth till all
could see the limitless expanse of
His LOVE, both here and beyond.

SPIRE ▮ BOOKS
Fleming H. Revell
A Division of Baker Book House
Grand Rapids, Michigan 49516

Copyright © 1978 by Richard E. Eby, D.O.
Published by Fleming H. Revell
a division of Baker Book House Company
P.O. Box 6287, Grand Rapids, MI 49516-6287
All rights reserved

ISBN: 0-8007-8489-8

Fourteenth printing, May 1995

Printed in the United States of America

Introduction

It is an honor to write this brief foreword for my friend and Christian brother, Dr. Eby. His outstanding ability as a successful physician in this area is widely known and recognized. However, this book is not about any single medical accomplishment Dr. Eby could so ably write or speak. Unlike most books, this subject matter did not originate in the author's mind; it is the story of God's grace to a practicing physician who died, went to heaven, and was sent back to perform a greater ministry than even before.

As I have previewed this script, I was repeatedly reminded and thankful to God, that this book is not an illusionary abstract. As a qualified physician he relates his actual experiences, with honesty and frankness. He saw the other side of death!

You will enjoy reading this book. To me it made things eternal seem so much more beautiful and understandable. A careful and prayerful study of its contents will bear out the fact that it is in harmony with God's Word.

As Dr. Eby's pastor, I can speak very highly for his Christian character and love for God. It is my personal prayer that many questioning hearts will find glorious release from the fear of death, and will understand better the promise of God found in I Corinthians 2:9: "Eye hath not seen, nor ear heard, neither hath entered into the heart of man the things that God hath prepared for them that love Him.

Rev. Harold C. Bither, Pastor
First Assembly of God Church
Pomona, California 91767

Acknowledgement

Now I know in part: but then I shall know and understand fully and clearly even in the same manner as I have been fully and clearly known and understood by God. I Corinthians 13:12, Amplified Bible

Occasionally one hears a story of a person who has experienced life after death. Many cases have been examined by psychologists and theologians alike. In every case the reality of life after death was evident.

Dr. Richard Eby has experienced this life after death and is a living testimony of things yet to come. His has been a unique journey in that God has allowed him to experience the glories of Paradise as well as the terrors of Hell.

However, his encounter with God's miraculous power doesn't begin here, but begins even at his birth. It is a story of miracle after miracle. The story of an individual being melted, molded, motivated, and moved by the Great Creator Himself. A living example of God and man, and how He cares for those who trust Him.

The story doesn't end here either, but continues as the life of the author goes on, still under the direction of God Himself.

God has allowed Dr. Eby to visit Paradise, but one day soon all those who believe upon the name of Jesus will experience this phenomena and the word *visit* will be changed to *eternity*.

We commend this book to you, realizing that it is not a book idly read and then discarded, but one that you will want to read over and over again and then share it with those you love.

Sam and Donna Starr
"Spirit Song" Member, TBN-TV
Covina, California 91723

Acknowledgement

Dr. Eby is a Christian gynecologist, Physician and Surgeon, who speaks the language of God's providential dealings with mankind. This book documents the sequential biography of one miracle after another, and it challenges the Faith of every individual to believe in a God who sovereignly directs, protects and carries out His designed plan for each person.

Caught Up into Paradise carries the dynamic message of a supernatural God whose "voice" is still clearly articulating that miracles have not ceased and that Faith is the agent of Change.

The last chapters of this book are most inspirational and underscore with absolute finality that God's ordained witnesses have been allowed to come back from the dead to vividly describe the beautiful Shekinah Paradise of the Redeemed and the stark horrors of rejecting the Word of God and being eternally separated from the presence of God forever!

THIS BOOK IS A MUST FOR EVERYONE!

Dan Kricorian
Senior Pastor
Calvary Church
6th and Grove Streets
Ontario, California 91764

Dedication

This story of God's caretaking
is being humbly told to
MAGNIFY THE MAJESTY
of the
FATHER ALMIGHTY
who receives our adoration and praise;
and of
JESUS THE CHRIST
who is worthy of all glory;
and of the
COMFORTER
whose Spirit restores and repairs
the communion between
THE HEAD
and
HIS BODY.

"HOW GREAT THOU ART"

In Appreciation

to my late

Beloved Parents

Their lives illustrated every Christian virtue of faith, hope, and charity. Their fruits of the Spirit enriched all whose paths intersected theirs.

They taught me about God: His earth; His heaven; and His people—some lost, some found; His life—eternal; His love—unbounded; His riches—unsearchable.

Dad and Mom admiring each other at his retirement banquet after 40 years as head of G.E. High Voltage Bushing Dept.

Foreword

It is the author's prayer that the reader will find in these pages the evidence of things not always seen and the substance of things he can still hope for. As little children holding God's Hand we can seek and find His Kingdom on earth as it is in heaven wherein each dwells within the other.

The author is using his personal experiences and memories to illustrate Divine truths in lives during the unbelievable human experiments of the twentieth century when God graciously tolerated mankind's abysmal foolishness and overt scorn. This generation has already survived four wars (a first, a second, a Korean, and a Viet Nam), two booms and a bust, political test tubes (NRA, WPA, CCC, CIA, ad nauseum), destructions and reconstructions, inflations and deflations, gas rationing and gas glutting, prohibition and whiskey advertising, aluminum pennies and paper scripts, communist attacks and communist endorsements, flag saluting and flag burning, gold banning and gold owning, blue laws and anti-blue laws, persecuting abortionists and protecting abortionists, arresting rapists and arresting the raped, condemning nicotine and underwriting it, banning churches but legalizing atheists, decrying halleluias but permitting hallucinogens . . . and God still forgivingly awaits our awakening!

Despite the foibles of its careless caretakers America is being given a second chance to become truly Beautiful:

God is touching hearts, holding hands, hovering over His children, and answering every answerable prayer. He wants us to be ready when He arrives! For this reason He is performing miracles, again and again.

CONTENTS

Part I

THE PITTSFIELD YEARS

Part II

THE MID-WEST YEARS

Part III

THE CALIFORNIA YEARS

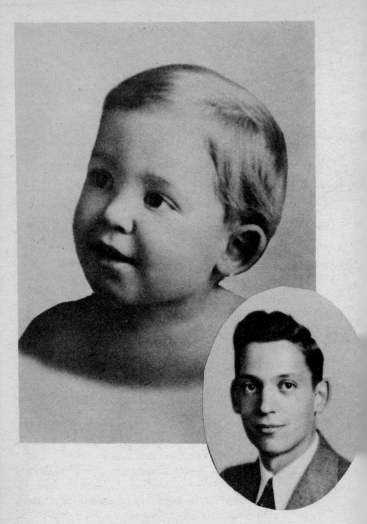

Jesus loves *me*—This I *know*:
He touched *me*!

Prologue to Paradise

> "And GRACE and PEACE from Jesus Christ who is
> the faithful witness, and the FIRST begotten of the
> dead, and the PRINCE of the kings of the earth . . . to
> Him be Glory and Dominion forever." Revelation 1:5

"Dick, you're dead!"

This seemed the most amazing, and yet the most normal and sensible, statement that I had ever uttered. I felt suddenly *at home.* I was instantly no longer in a strange world, as earth had seemed so often, but in Paradise *personally prepared* for my arrival. The Peace was overwhelmingly ecstatic and *instantly mine.*

Here I was, unaware of how I had died and left the old body somewhere. I had no memory of earth. In a *twinkling of an eye* my memory had been erased, and my body replaced with the most exquisite mind and new body imaginable. I gasped with glee. God and His handiwork were everywhere. I began to inspect my new "abode" obviously prepared just for me to enjoy until the final trump would sound. I was home at last. What joy!

It has been five years already since that sweltering day in Chicago when satan pushed me from the balcony in another attempt to close my mouth and still my hands. In that split second Jesus caught me up for a glimpse of His "mansion" prepared for that moment alone. I find it difficult even now to phrase into English words the description of the total ecstasy and boundless love which pervade Paradise. The instant release from mortal shortcomings is really indescribable (St. Paul says, "unutterable").

Before I can describe my mansion in heaven (John 14:2), I must relate how God maneuvered this little child of His in preparation for such a day. Through my story, I pray that you can compare your own preparation, whether inside or outside His Will, and that you can clearly see how your Maker molds, then re-molds, each earthly event for our use on high. Let us look back with praise upon each of His hand-crafted days in our lives. Then His purpose for our lives can come into focus. And *that* picture is suddenly and gloriously magnificent!

QUESTION:

"Surely your turning of things upside down shall be esteemed as the potter's clay: for shall the work say of him who made it, He made me not? Or shall the thing framed say of him that framed it, He had no understanding?" Isaiah 29:16

ANSWER:

"Behold! I have graven thee upon the palms of my hands." Isaiah 49:16

Part I

THE
PITTSFIELD
YEARS

MIRACLE 1

In the Berkshires

"And God said, Let Us make man in Our image, after Our likeness: and let them have dominion over the fish . . . And God blessed them." Gen. 1:26, 28

In June each rosey dawn tiptoes gently across the glazed waters of Pontoosuc Lake. Faint ringlets spread and die as luckless gnats become breakfast for unseen perch. Sounds are rare; just the occasional damp splash of an early bird (dressed like a kingfisher) scooping a surprised minnow from a ripple. Delicate fingers of light inch downward from the wooded heights of the Housatonics, hesitating in the cool valleys to caress the sleepy birches. Dawn seems reluctant to awaken this gentle place in New England's Berkshires from its dream of peace on earth, but it must. Nature stirs, and a new day is suddenly reborn out of darkness!

Thus it was in western Massachusetts in the year of our Lord 1912, when God had selected a young engineer and his loving wife to become my parents. They did not know it yet! Instead they were vacationing at this lake, named by the Mohawks "the watering place of the white-tailed deer." It reminded them of their childhood scenery in Michigan where they were raised on nearby farms close to many small lakes. Each had grown up watching the hand of God at work in the land, the lilies, the lakes, and the lives of His people.

Dad was born in the front room of this centennial home. Seventy years later we see his uncle still collecting hickory nuts to use in the Church "bake sales" down the road.

This serious-minded son of a frontier judge learned to interpret whatever he saw as proof of a world of law and order, one which only an Omniscient Creator could have invented to replace chaos. The school teacher's daughter saw the same scenes as proof of the incomparable artistry, grace, and harmony of a world which her loving Father arranged for every lamb in His flock. They first met as teenagers in the peach orchard on her father's farm and the miracle of love had enmeshed them instantly. After a long lonely wait for him to graduate from Colorado University, and move to Pittsfield, they married.

Here at the Lake he could fish for a "big one" while she sat on the cottage porch and dreamed about her baby boy due next September.

It was already Thursday morning and Gene was across the lake. He had spotted a little cove beyond Indian Island where several pickerel weeds were swaying convulsively as an invisible fish tore dragonfly larvae from resisting stems. He rowed into the cove this morning ever so quietly before any shadows could disclose his presence, so he could catch that "big one" for his sleeping "Angel" back at the cottage!

The No. 0 hook with a shiny minnow was quietly dropped overboard. In obedient panic it darted downward among the sleeping stems seeking a suitable leaf for shelter. Gene sat back and waited. What more could a man want? God's world was at peace; the waves were stilled; a fish would soon bite; and next Fall he would be a father. He looked up at the fading morning star and whispered:

"The heavens declare the glory of God, and the firmament showeth His handiwork; day unto day uttereth speech and night unto night showeth knowledge . . ."

His voice trailed off as his mind finished reciting this poetry of praise.

God was listening — and getting ready to reveal His love in an unexpected development that day.

Back at the cottage where the kerosene lamp had gone out, Mable awoke suddenly with a strange pain. She reached over and patted across the empty bed, "Naturally," she smiled; "Eugene had said he would leave before daybreak to catch a prize fish for our Friday dinner!" Her hand slid back across her rounded abdomen. Strange. It was now tender and firm. Not at all like yesterday when it was comfortable to feel two little heels and hands exploring the inner darkness.

She must pray for her fisherman to return: she always felt secure when he was around. Certainly *these* pains would stop. After all, this was still June. Only last week the doctor had said, "Enjoy your vacation! Your labor day won't be till Fall." If only Eugene would catch a fish soon, she mused. "I wonder how God will tell him to come back right away?. . . ."

The rusty mosquito netting around the sleeping porch began to filter the tinted sunlight across a weathered sign above the porch doorway. She noted its whittled letters, "CASTLE WINDY," and lay back and smiled: "God has stilled the wind this morning just so Gene can row easily back home."

She picked up her worn Bible from a varnished apple crate beside the brass headboard. The glow hit its worn pages where it fell open at the marker; for months she had been reading this favorite passage. She so wanted a son. The country doctors back in Michigan had warned her that she should never plan on having a baby.

She felt her abdomen tighten again. "When this child grows up," she told herself, "I will tell him about that friendly Indian medicine man who heard God talk about me the day I died for a while on the farm."

A shaft of brighter light hit the page so she could read the circled verse, telling of Hannah who had talked to God about her own pregnancy. There it was (I Samuel 1:11) just as though she had said it herself:

> "And she vowed a vow and said, 'O Lord of Hosts, if Thou wilt indeed look upon the affliction of your handmaid, and remember me, and not forget thine handmaid, but will give unto thine handmaid a man-

child, then I will give him unto the Lord all the days
of his life. . . ."

If Hannah's vow had been honored, she wondered, why
wouldn't He do the same for an engineer's wife? And
wasn't it only right to share an unborn baby with the
Lord?

She remembered another exciting promise in the first
chapter of Jeremiah where the Lord spoke to the prophet
saying:

**"Before I formed thee in the belly I knew thee; and
before thou camest forth out of the womb I sanctified
thee. . . ."**

Quietly she pondered: "Only our loving Lord could plan
like that. He makes us His children long before we even
get here! It must be that God uses mothers' bodies to
shape and carry His children for Him. How sensible! I
don't believe any mother is smart enough to put a baby's
parts together by herself. It's lucky that mothers can leave
this baby business to Him . . . I wish Eugene would hurry
back! Please, God!"

A rolling wake formed behind the row boat, as
Eugene bent his muscle back against the long ash oars.
Wouldn't Mable be surprised to see him back so soon! He
would tell her how he had pulled up the unwanted minnow, then quietly paddled forward among the pink lily
blossoms. Then the unexpected happened! The water at
the prow had exploded (it seemed deafening in the still
air), and over the side like a fat writhing snake flopped the
most surprised pickerel in the lake. It had been napping
under the lilypads when the wooden prow nudged him
into flight. His leaping arc had landed him in the boat
where he now lay wrapped in a wet gunny sack.

Eugene's heart sang; the Lord is with me this morning! Instead of fishing all day to get a prize for his "little mother," he was already speeding back in the slanting rays of the dawn. Hopefully she would be at the dock to meet him. Then they could spend the day hand-in-hand hiking through the sloping fields of wild berries and buttercups that rimmed the miles of shoreline. He shook the sweat from his glasses and doubled his strokes.

From her bed on the porch Mable was anxiously watching for an answer to prayer. And there it was. The approaching shaft of ripples headed for the dock. God had somehow told Eugene to come back early. She worshipped and wondered; "Just how did God tell him? Just when my pains are getting worse?"

Surely God was smiling as He watched His chosen pickerel obey its orders to bring the fisherman back to land. He was enjoying His strategy already, and He had much more planned!

MIRACLE 2

It's a Boy

"And He said unto me, My grace is sufficient for thee. . . ." II Corinthians 12:9

The rest of that day was a blur. Somehow Gene had swapped his fish at a neighboring farmhouse in return for a horse and buggy which he had left tethered at the trolley station at the lower end of the lake. They somehow survived the jolting 12-mile streetcar ride to town, and walked the last two blocks to the House of Mercy. The white-starched nurse noted that the cramps were every five minutes. "You're lucky," she said, "the doctor just happens to be upstairs hosting the Convention of Massachusetts Obstetricians. If you had waited until tomorrow he would have been in Boston." Mable glanced at Eugene's relaxing face; after all, hadn't Jesus promised, "I will never leave thee nor forsake thee?"

By evening it happened. Dr. Roberts "caught" the little bundle of premature life. He left its purplish form on a warm water bottle until his visiting guest-doctors upstairs could examine the sure-to-die body. They all agreed: best not tell the mother it had lived at all. Why make her suffer two disappointments the same day? She certainly must have known on the way here it could not survive . . . (No one on duty should tell her anything different). They then advised the husband to prepare his tired young wife to face "the facts."

Back in her room, Mable was hearing an unseen Jesus whispering through her ether-blurred brain. "I am giving your tiny boy back into your care because we *both* love him so much. Remember? I am still the Resurrection and the Life. Let not your heart be troubled . . . I too believe in miracles." She listened and slept while the nurses wondered about her being so calm all day.

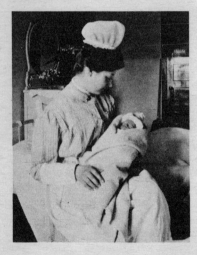

Born to live. One week old and going home.

A week later, in a cotton-lined shoebox, wearing inch-long blue-booties, feather-weight Richard arrived home to face the future. The grace of Jesus had proven quite sufficient already. The baby couldn't know that God had planned to take him to Heaven for a visit sixty years later. Now Richard's little mew meant one thing: rush the milk, I need to grow fast!

MIRACLE 3

Kitchen Table Healing

". . . For I say unto you that in heaven their angels do always behold the face of my Father. . . ." Matt. 18:10

Mable never doubted that her baby would grow. But it did seem painfully slow as she held him close during the chilling nights of his first New England winter. Her fervent prayers were for added strength. (She told him years later that he used to smile in his sleep when his private angel heard her prayers).

By Spring he was a squawling skinny ten-pounder ready to attack the next spoonful of cream-of-wheat, although his attentive doctor, a lady D.O. with a compassionate heart and delicate fingers, had misgivings. She had detected a growing mass in his lower abdomen. Her consultants were openly pessimistic: "Best do surgery," they warned, "Soon!"

Gene and Mable knelt again and sought guidance. The answer came through her parents, in Los Angeles, whose urgent desire was to see Richard lest "Grandma's" illness should take her away. The baby could be operated on in California. And so it happened. A leather satchel was outfitted as a portable bed for the long trip. Dad bought a rail ticket for two (a rattan seat next to a pot-bellied stove) on a swaying Santa Fe coach. This was their "home" for the week's crossing of America's young frontier. Every morning the steam-moistened soot from the "puffer-belly" locomotive blackened their noses, but who cared? Every mile California was getting closer; at last Cajon Pass and the screeching of iron wheels stopping at Pasadena. None the worse for wear, Richard in his satchel had made the trip and awaited the morrow.

Ready to leave for a satchel trip and healing adventure in California. Sept., 1913.

Grandma bared the kitchen table to cover it with newspapers as the two doctors scrubbed at the iron sink. The senior surgeon from Germany had arrived yesterday to lecture at the County Hospital auditorium. He laid a sterile sheet over the tiny body now snoring under an ether mask, and scowled at the egg-sized lump under his knife. He could hear the mother's quiet prayer-for-skill from the parlor.

In all his years he had not seen a growth quite like this, he told his assistant as he waved a fly away and hurried his closure. He remarked that no scrawny baby like this one would be expected to survive. Tomorrow he would learn the kind of malignancy that could grow this fast. He also wondered what good was prayer for a year-old kid weighing so little?

Then the bandages went on and Richard started screaming. Never had he smelled a stink like that ether! And besides, somebody must have pinched him down there! "Hey, what goes? Can't you pick on someone your own size?"

The moon had nearly set when a bone-tired mother finished her love letter to Eugene, telling of the long trip, the kitchen-table surgery, and her answers to prayer. She even predicted that the "Malignancy" would prove benign (and she was right). Maybe the doctors would someday believe in her Healer. "Anything is possible," she wrote, "if only you *let* Him help when you ask!" Her pen fell to the floor, and she was asleep.

In the next room the incision was already healing. Little did the young assisting doctor realize as he checked the bandage that morning that he, as a new College President, 24 years later would confer a doctorate degree on this very infant. Neither of them could possibly know what God knew: that 49 years later He would arrange for the baby to become a College President also. If either had known, both would have scoffed. So God didn't tell them.

There was ample time on His calendar for many developments. After all, He was in the healing business too.

MIRACLE 4

Breath of Life

"For My strength is made perfect in weakness. . . ."
II Corinthians 12:9

Richard could walk quite steadily by Christmas. He was also learning (the hard way) about what happens when little fingers grab the hot oven door where the good smells were escaping. It was no cooler when he touched the polished nickel skirt around the potbellied stove that warmed the sitting room. He really wanted to investigate that yellow flame in the oil lamp where father sat to prepare his Sunday School lessons, but it was too high to reach.

In fact, the only good thing about being two feet tall was the ease of falling to the floor. He was already nearly there!

It seemed that everyone who came to Castle Windy wanted to lift him up and kiss him. The kissing was terribly slobbery, but it was otherwise worthwhile: from shoulder height he could spot a host of goodies on top of tables and dressers! He catalogued them for future reference just in case life someday got dull next to the rag rugs.

When he was four, something wrong was happening at Castle Windy. Mother wouldn't let him play with his 9 month-old brother Robert. Robert had become "No.

1 companion" ever since the snow outside had become too deep for his regular companions to play like they did in the summers. A strange man with a black bag had come three times and thumped Robert's chest and listened through a rubber hose. When he talked to Mother she cried, and Father turned pale. He said funny words like *Pneumonia* and *dying*. He said to leave the baby on the screened porch where the blowing snow would fight the fever.

At the next visit he said, "It'll be tonight." This time Father sobbed and held Mother ever so tight. Then he straightened up and cranked the new box on the wall, three shorts and a long; a pause, then, "Pastor . . . Gene at the lake . . . Doc just left. There's no chance . . . Both lungs solid now. I can't get to Prayer meeting tonight: Mother needs me, you know, it's especially hard on her. Please ask our people to pray tonight that she will have strength to bear up. We praise Jesus for letting us have our little boy for almost a year." The tiny bell in the box tolled again as he hung up.

The crunch of boots on frozen snow disturbed that Wednesday night's silence. The "faithful" were collecting at the lamplit Baptist Church in Morningside. Word had spread fast that miles away at the Lake, Gene and Mable were keeping a death watch over little Robert. Someone fired up the church stove. Gertrude loosened her cold fingers on her upright "grand," and Rev. Leach arrived to start the singing: "My Faith Is Built On Nothing Less Than Jesus' Love And Righteousness . . .", "And tonight, Dear Lord, we ask a special favor; unless You need that little baby real bad in Heaven in Your loving arms, please heal him *right now* and leave him down here! Either way, we will praise You. But couldn't You use him

Harry C. Leach, D.D.

someday in Your work if You simply breathe *New Life* into him now? Thank you, Jesus!"

The pastor's watch showed 8:30 PM as he wiped his tears and announced the closing hymn. He then tarried to see that all lamps were blown out, and that the fire in the stove was safely banked for the night. It was warm and quiet at last in the sanctuary, and he instinctively closed his eyes and said from memory:

> "Bless the Lord, Oh my soul, and all that is within me bless His Holy Name . . . and FORGET NOT ALL HIS BENEFITS"

Benefits? Could they be the prophecy for tonight? Oh my. There goes the phone again: "Yes . . . ?"

The distant voice on the line was hard to understand, familiar but so excited. "Harry. Harry . . . pardon me . . . Pastor . . . Robert is alive and well! It's a miracle . . .

"Family Bible Hour" on screen porch in 1915 where prayer healed baby Robert 6 months after this snapshot at Castle Windy.

We were sitting there . . . by that little lifeless body . . . when the parlor clock struck the half hour after 8, and the crib shook! Robert suddenly rubbed his eyes, and sat up, and cried for milk . . . His fever is gone. . . . God has healed him! (Pause) "What time was it when you prayed for him tonight?"

Pastor Leach smiled knowingly through his tears: "You already know the exact moment, Gene."

Thursday morning the doctor came again. When he left the cottage, he was shaking his head slowly: "Any-

Sixty years later Robert sits at his 100th Artisan Organ hand-crafted for a customer.

one with brains knows that a baby that age dies with double pneumonia. What went wrong with my predictions? Do his parents know something I don't? ... Can it be. . . ?"

Interlude
Playtime

"And the child grew, . . . and the grace of God was upon Him. . . ." Luke 2:40

Then came happy days for the boys! Naturally, it was church on Sunday where those "kissin' wimmen" would hug and pat "the little dears" who lived "way out at the Lake," and would wonder why "baby" Robert was already outgrowing his older brother who was "cute but puny." But the good part of Sunday was what happened

Robert and Richard dressed up for Church.

when someone laid hands on the organ and made it sound wonderful! Robert's feet would tap the maple pew, and Richard's hands would mimic the songleader (at least till Mother would reach over and whisper, "Boys! Remember you're in *CHURCH!*")."OK. But someday can we do it ourselves?"

The rest of each week was hilarious. Like twins they would romp through the blackeyed susans down to the dock and lie for minutes peering through the warped boards at the lazy sunfish. . . . "They must be singing, just like the folks do at church. All their faces are opening and closing like a choir!" Then they were off to chase a cottontail which had ventured out for a drink.

Flopping into the warm grass was also fun; it gave time to look at clouds and dream. . . . We'll probably be late for our chores; better gather a bouquet of forget-me-nots and yellow mustard blossoms; Mother hugs us even when we're late if we say "I love you" and give her flowers! Somehow she knows when to spank us though. She must have eyes in the back of her head, 'cause when we wait to disobey her till she is not around, she still knows. She says she loves us "real special" because God nearly took us away from her and Daddy. She says she will pay Jesus back by helping us to grow "upright" instead of naughty. She loves her Jesus (He's the God people tried to kill once, but He rose right up out of the cemetery and walked back to His favorite lake to eat fish with His friends.) He loves little children so much that He wants us around Him in heaven. That's where each of our angels is talking to Him right now. Mama's angel must be real old! Do you suppose she was ever a child? Maybe she was sick once and Jesus made *her* well. Funny. She and Daddy act like there is another "father" around our house. After we catch that red butterfly over there, we'll ask her. Hey, I can find prettier flowers than you can. Look, there's a toad. Let's take it to Mama!

MIRACLE 5

The Voice of Thy Thunder

"And then shall the priest ... take ... birds and cedarwood, and scarlet, and hissop ... and dip them in the blood. ..." Lev. 14:6

Each thunderstorm brought excitement to Castle Windy. Naturally no one could sleep through the noise. The tongue-in-groove walls rattled with each Boom, and the window panes popped dried putty onto the floor. Luckily for the boys, the narrow stairs to their bedroom passed a window facing the western flint-tipped Taconic mountains where those blinding tongues of flame darted

Castle Windy at Lake Pontoosuc. "Lightning Window" upstairs faces west.

from the pitch-black heavens. Mama would pile pillows on the risers so the shivering boys could see the 'show' over the windowsill. It became a contest to guess when the next "fireworks" would explode. (With her so near there could be no danger even if it was scary!)

"You see," she would whisper, "God's world needs fire and water so people and every living thing can keep warm, and drink, and grow. So many people nowdays forget about His power that He has to make a big noise to get their attention once in a while. Long ago a King, called David, told his people that God made the heavens to declare His glory. Now, Let's count how many seconds it takes before they declare it again! One . . . two . . . three . . ."

When the count reached "thirty" it meant that the fireworks had passed by. The distant boom of rolling thunder became drowned out by the storm's trailing edge of pelting rain against the noisy windows. The boys were excited since they knew "story time" had arrived. (Mama knew better than to expect them to fall off to sleep without an interlude of tales from her past.)

"Tonight, boys, I have a special story to tell you; this time about Indians. Those are the people who first lived in this big country before the white man came over the ocean and made them live together on camp-grounds called "reservations." They loved the thunder and lightning and believed that their Great Spirit spoke from the sky too."

There was a flurry of activity getting their pillows back on the couch in neat order, then racing each other to be first into a bed where Mother would hold one on each side and finish her story.

"When I was a little girl on the farm somewhere near a place called Dowagiac, I came home one day from the little red schoolhouse where a big bell hung on top. I felt very sick. Your Grandma put me to bed because I was hot and dizzy and could not walk a straight line. Daddy sat up with me during the night. That was the last I remembered, for quite a while. He told me later, that in the morning he saddled up Whoa-Nellie and rode her to Elkhart looking for a doctor who came the next day as fast as he could find his way across the fields. He told your Grandpa to go to the next farm where the carpenter would help him make a coffin my size, because I was already mostly dead, and there was no hope. When he got back with the coffin tied to his saddle, he found the local Indian Medicine Man waiting with two warriors on their ponies. The Chief asked him, "Where is Pretty-girl-that-runs-to-meet-us? Great Spirit told me come see her." They dismounted and went inside. Grandma was crying over my stiff grey body on the little bed. "She's gone," Grandpa exclaimed.

88 year-old Great-grandpa Engle tells Carol about Indian Medicine Man who annointed her grandma with "goo" in 1897.

The Chief tapped him on the shoulder. "No die! Great Spirit say, 'Let medicine man use sacred medicine. He bring girl back. When Great Sun rise in morning, little girl want water. You give her some! I go now, get Indian medicine for Pretty-girl." He bowed and backed out of the door.

"My parents told me later that they were reluctant to let the Indian do anything to me when I was already stiff and apparently dead. But Grandpa realized he was the President's Commissioner to these Indians (that means he was the special white man to whom they brought their troubles), and he must not offend them if he wanted their respect. Besides, he wanted them someday to love the God who made us people red or white! So he gave permission to the Indians to get their sacred medicine. Just before sunset the Chief rode back into our front yard carrying a red pot full of black 'goo.' ("Goo" consisted of a mixture of swamp herbs, roots and barks boiled and mixed with blood of birds, frogs, and snakes to make a black liniment for use by a "Medicine Man" only.) They told me that he rubbed it all over me, except my nose, and rode away.

"When the sun came up Grandpa heard the Indian pony gallop into the front yard just when I cried out for water! (He cried too.) The Chief had another potful of 'goo' that he spread all over me again. He told my father this time: "Great Spirit talk to me on horse. Say girl want food when Great Sun go down tonight. He say feed her then! And away he rode."

Mother swung off the bed. "More, Mommy, more. Did you live?" "Boys, you figure that out while I get some milk and cookies like we used to give our Indian friends every time they came to see me afterwards. . . .

"Now, to go on with the story . . . Watch those crumbs; they'll tickle! Well, that evening the little girl ate some food, and could hear the Chief tell her Daddy that the next day the Great Spirit would make her walk by sunset. And I did!

"Boys, we have a word for things we can't explain; it's 'MIRACLE.' The doctor called me a real miracle. Years later he explained that I had a kind of brain fever that the city doctors were calling "Infantile Paralysis." Other such children had died in hospitals even with pills and hot packs. I learned that the Indians' *Great Spirit* is the same God who can do miracles for us. When you learn to read you will find that the Great Spirit was first called 'Jehovah,' and He made this earth and the lightning and thunder that we watched tonight. He even gives little boys happy dreams. Now, it's time to tell Jesus Thank You for the lovely rain and for the milk and cookies, and for Daddy and Mama. Goodnight . . . Sleep tight."

They fell asleep, wondering if they would ever see a real Indian or the Great Spirit. They would thank him for Mama's goo!

MIRACLE 6

A New Heart for My People

> "Give Thy servant an understanding heart to judge
> Thy people that I may discern between good and
> bad." I Kings 3:9

If the boys had not been so sleepy she would have
told them about the fierce hatred which the Michigan Indians, Potowatomi's and other tribes, had held against the
white man for 2 hundred years. When their beautiful rolling hills and fishing waters had been 'stolen' by the gun-
shooting invaders with the pale faces, they had felt seriously threatened. Their teepee villages had been destroyed
and their sacred hunting grounds invaded. Their women
had been abused and their children killed. Whole Indian
villages had been wiped out. Any survivors were driven
further westward, completely away from the "Great
Waters" that surrounded their peaceful land of Michi-
gam-wah.

In desperation they had fought back in the only way
they knew. When the daily convoys of buckboards and
covered wagons had streamed westward from Detroit
toward Illi-noih ("Land of warriors") they had tried to
ambush the leaders and throw the wagon trains into rout.
It had only worked for a while. Then came the uniformed
troops with their "bang-sticks" that killed at a distance.

And their resistance was broken for all time.

No longer would the smoke rise quietly from the tee-pee's cooking fire: nor would the chanted hymns of the Medicine Man comfort the rocking form of a sobbing mother with her sick babe in arms. The hunters could no longer rehearse tales of the valor required to bring a great moose out of the forest to feed a snow-bound clan during the long winter's freeze. Their traditional prayers to the Great Spirit were prohibited by their captors. Long-festering fears distilled into innate hatred or contempt for the "laws of the land."

Into this frontier of racial disrespect Mable had been innocently born of God-fearing parents. To neighboring farmers the Engle's seemed colorblind, without ability to realize that red and white skins should have nothing in common. Some believed that the white man had been created by God with infinite intelligence; the Indian had descended from some ape-like ancestor with a feather in his greasy hair. Was it not the duty of the European settlers to rid God's land of these remnants of a damned and doomed inferior race? What greater purpose had God ordained for the newcomers into this promised land of rich soil and lumber and living things?

It had been a wild frontier before the mild-mannered Engle's established their peach farm in the clearing two miles from the red school house. A few years later Frank had lost his little son when the four-year old excitedly chased a curious fawn into the neighboring pond one day, but Frank had prayed; and God told him to stay in his "wilderness," and teach and work and trust. So he took the post of schoolhouse principal, and the job of teaching English, and the appointment as Commissioner to the Potawatomi people down by the creek.

"Why, God," he would ask as he laid his wearied body on the rope mattress at midnight, "do you ask so much of me?" The answer was always the same: "I never ask too much. You will know My Rest someday when you look back."

If the boys had been still awake Mable would have finished her story with a spark of pardonable pride in her voice. She would have related how she became a school teacher in that same red school house, and later at the High school in Dowagiac. There she had studied from history books and noted that the end of the Indian rebellions in western Michigan had coincided with her father's term as Commissioner. She learned that the Medicine Men had some mysterious way of "telegraphing" their messages over hills and valleys in no time at all, and supposed that the word of her "miracle" recovery had been spread throughout the clans across Michigan. The fact that her father had permitted his prized daughter to be treated by their "Shaman" with Indian Medicines had likely been widely discussed around the campfires. Such an unexpected token of respect must have restored their lost sense of dignity.

"Who knows?", she pondered. "Did Jesus permit my little brother to drown and me to nearly die and my Daddy to speak kindly to the Shaman, just so there would be peace between the red and white people? Does God go to such lengths to show that He wants us to love each other as He loves us? Do His *hard* lessons shape us for unknown chores ahead? I think so. That's what He says in His Word:

"I work All things together for good for them that love Me. . . ." Romans 8:28

MIRACLE 7

If You Will But Believe

"How often would I have gathered thy children together, even as a hen gathereth her chickens under her wings. . . . ! Matthew 25:37

Grandma was still alive in California but had not yet seen brother Robert: "It didn't seem right"—especially now that they had a guest-house at the big ranch where Grandpa had hired on to tend the orchards. Besides it was beautiful in this San Fernando Valley, year round! Mother swallowed the bait: it wasn't really right to deny Grandma a visit from her newest grandson. "We'll be there for Christmas" she wrote, and licked the one-cent stamp.

What fun it was for the boys to ride the swaying Pullman especially when the porter laid the two seats together and made a bunk! Then the big thrill—when he pulled down the ceiling and out came an "upstairs bed," and thick green curtains with a ladder underneath. At dusk they would squirm out of their clothes below the little round flickering light and put them in the long fishnet stretched above the cotton mattress. Then Mother would say prayers and tuck them in, a head at each end so they wouldn't talk all night! That didn't stop them from playing "Toesy" though; it made them giggle quietly to think of how they were putting one over on Mom!

Each day the train stopped 3 times for everyone to get off at a "dining room" with wooden benches. Mother said it was called a "Harvey House." Wrinkled old Indian ladies on red blankets sat outside holding up beads and bracelets with blue stones. They pointed to cardboard signs that read "Beads 25¢" or "Bracelets 60¢." Mother bought a watch fob for Daddy for 20¢: it said "YUMA" in colored beads.

The boys wondered why the Indians didn't talk much, and Mother explained that they had no schools to go to like "our people" had back home. They'd have to think about that later, because the steam whistle just then blew three times, for everyone to hurry back. "Alllll-uhhh—Boooooo-oo-aaaa—rrrd—ah." Tomorrow they would see Grandma and play on the farm.

They found the animals especially exciting. (In Sunday School last year Richard had learned about Noah's animals in the Big Boat. How happy Noah must have been to wake up in the morning and hear them all talking!) The rooster in the barn would croak (is that the right word?) before the sun rose. The cows and horses were scarey, they were so big; but the baby chicks were just right. Soft and warm and squeaky, like wiggley cotton balls, only yellow. He fell in love with the dozens of them hatching under bushes and old crates wherever their pecking mothers hid them. The day after Christmas he awoke to see snow on the ground and ran shivering downstairs to warm up by the old iron range in the large kitchen. Mother was cooking oatmeal with raisins in it.

Mr. Dawley (he had owned the farm for 50 years, Mother said) sat head in hands: "Not for years have I seen a sudden freeze like this," . . . he was telling Mable. "Your father had the groves readied for a heavy harvest, and now most of the fruit is lost! Even my baby chicks are all frozen stiff; I didn't find a single one alive this morning. . . ."

Richard stopped rigid in the doorway: his little chicks dead? Could he help Mr. Dawley gather them up? . . . Please? "Well, yes, if you bundle up warm and stay close to his side," Mother cautioned.

It was a sad search. Under boxes and trees lay little downie bodies stiff as ice. When the 10 gallon pail in Mr. Dawley's left hand was half filled with lifeless forms he pointed back to the house: "Run in the house, Richard, and get warm while I dig a hole and bury these chickens." His hand patted the hesitating boy's bottom. "But, Mister, can't I play with them in the house till you finish digging the hole? They were my friends. Please? I won't hurt them." He couldn't help smiling. Why not? Where could one find cheaper toys on a cold morning?

The oven was standing open. To Richard's delight an empty cookie tin lay on the table, greased for later use. He could now see if his Sunday School teacher had been honest when he told that *big story* about how God made people out of dirt, and then held them lovingly in His hands and breathed His breath on them to make them come alive. The teacher said that God made every living thing that way; and when He came back to earth later He proved He could do it again by touching the sick or dead people and making them alive and well. OK. Let's see if it works that way!

The only hands and breath that Richard had in the kitchen were his own; so he cupped each little ball of feathers in his two palms and blew. Puff. Puff. Puff. Then onto the cookie tin and into the oven they went: one by one until the pail was empty. He sat and watched. *Nothing happened*! So he closed the oven door. Maybe God worked better in the dark by Himself. Maybe God was like Mother: she usually said, "While Mama is working, you go play in the other room. When I'm through, I'll tell you."

Ancient Mr. Dawley set his shovel down and pushed open the backdoor. "Well, Sonny, have you finished playing? The hole's all dug but you won't need to come this time. I'll bury them myself." He looked into the pail and straightened up. "Now what have you done? Hid 'em? Swallowed 'em? You young-uns are a caution."

"Course not, Mister. Jesus is warming them in the oven. See . . . ?"

Richard proudly pulled the warm door downward, absolutely sure of what he would find. "See? My teacher was right. You just have to hold them and blow on them and they get well!" Staggering and tumbling over one another to escape the hot darkness, a pailful of cheeping chicks fled out of the oven, fell, bounced, and headed around the room. Only one lay still. "That one Jesus kep for His-self! You can have the others, Mister! Aren't you glad?"

Yes, a stunned old farmer was glad. But he wouldn't dare tell his neighbors how his batch of chicks had come through the freeze. They would just laugh. Some things you just keep to yourself when you don't know the answer, he decided.

Richard would never quite forget that morning either. In his 5 year-old mind there kept churning the embryo of an idea: if Jesus who made little boys could use their hands to make dead chickies live again, why wouldn't He do it for people? Maybe this Jesus Man would get *people* well even *before* they got dead if he had a boy's hands to do it for Him.

Why not? Wouldn't it be fun someday to have a black bag like that doctor-man who had come and told Daddy that Robert was dying? Instead, Daddy had explained that Robert got well when those Church people prayed for Jesus to touch Baby brother. Why didn't that doctor learn how to pray too? Seems like it would help a lot. "I'll ask Mama if it would be alright for me to try it someday." It shouldn't be hard: I'll get a black bag somewhere and try it myself! Oh yes, I'll have to get a watch on a chain too. My doctor has to look at his when he holds my hand. . . . I'll have to practice frowning too. . . . I must remember to say, "It will take a little more time. . . ." Our doctor says that a lot.

MIRACLE 8

Haven of Rest

"The angel of Jehovah encampeth round about them that fear Him, and delivereth them." Psa. 34:7

Growing up was fun at the Lake. The boys would not realize till later when they raised their own families just what work and sacrifice was required of their parents to provide such a wholesome environment in this post-war economy of the 20's. Yet never did they hear a word of complaint about the extra work of living beyond the outskirts of town where electricity and piped water and oiled roads had not yet reached.

Instead the family became a close-knit foursome. It was fun to rise early to split wood for the cookstove with its water-well in the end; then Mother would dip out steaming washwater into the zinc tub with its corrugated scrub board. In the winter, the same stove became surrounded at night with stiffly frozen long underwear and dresses brought in from the icy clothesline. The kerosene lamps cast exciting flickers that made shadows behind the garments dance like ghosts. The boys would huddle in the warmth and giggle with imagination as the melting arms and legs abruptly bent and collapsed into lifeless heaps of laundry on the floor.

Sometimes Mother or Dad would join them on the rug and explain that people became like winter laundry once in a while . . . all frozen and ghostlike. "Hard-hearted" was one word for it. When they got that way they were of little value, just like frozen clothing. "What can be done about it?" Richard would ask. His parents, wise in the art of school-teaching, would answer with a question, "What do we do with the frozen clothes?" "Well, we warm them up around the stove and they get soft. . . . Oh, I see. When people turn cold they get melted by being around somebody warm . . . Is that why people shake hands and hug, to warm each other? That must be what love is for. Is that right?" "Of course. By the way, it's your turn to clean the lamp chimneys so we can see to read a love story about Ruth and Boaz."

All too often Dad had to go somewhere. His Company, called the "G.E.," kept sending him around the country to tell other engineers how to invent and build electrical equipment to transmit high voltages ("something like lightning, only along wires," Dad had explained once.) When he was gone, the round-bottom boat would rock lonesomely at the dock, and the garden weeds would outgrow the beets and Hubbard squash. Two robins and a grosbeak family used his absence for stealing strawberries after consuming the few remaining cherries where Mother had hung Mason jar lids in the tree, quite in vain!

"Chores" was one of Dad's favorite words; he "assigned" them before leaving on each trip. Whichever boy got the "Whoa-Dick" chore felt rewarded. The horse was getting old, but he still needed hay and oats and rubbing with a wire brush. His hide felt so warm and friendly. It wasn't really work to take care of him, because he always lowered his head and rubbed his upper lip against their heads and said Thankyou in horse-talk that boys could understand.

"Whoa Dick" waits at the gate for little Dick to say "Gidup."

They were sure that it wasn't Whoa-Dick's fault two years ago when a little piece of steel had broken off his shoe while having a shoenail replaced. It pierced Dad's left eye. The doctors had said that they would have to remove the eyeball, but Dad had said NO! He simply had to have two eyes to do his exacting work at the G.E. . . . besides, his Bible said that his Christ had received stripes long ago for the healing of anyone who would accept it, and that was that. The doctors then called it a "miracle" when his eye quickly healed; so had Dad. However, Whoa-Dick always seemed more gentle after that, as though he remembered Dad's hurt.

The hard chores always grew tiresome when Dad was delayed an extra day. Watering, and weeding, and "worming cabbage leaves" got to be old stuff in a hurry. Cleaning ashes out of the cookstove, and wiping the lamp chimneys each morning wasn't fun like exploring woodchuck holes and climbing trees to look in bird nests. One job was fun, though: making beds with Mother's help. The sheets smelled so sweet after hanging in the sun; and it was a contest to see who could smooth out the wrinkles real tight, then with a giggle bounce off the bed, dart downstairs, out the door, and down to the dock where a can of worms was waiting. Dad should be back soon, and they would catch him a punkinseed, a big one!

But this time Dad didn't come back soon. Instead, Mother got a phone call that he was delayed and would be home in 2 days on the Boston & Albany coach out of Grand Central. He would explain later. They knew that this trip had taken him somewhere near Georgia to inspect a new power plant in the Appalachian mountains. They wondered what had happened as they sat waiting in the buggy at the streetcar station. Whoa-Dick flicked flies with his thinning tail, and peered pensively down the receding tracks toward town.

It was always exciting. After the hugging, they had klop-klopped back the dusty road along the lakeshore sending clouds of colored butterflies off the buttercups and milkweeds between the wheeltracks. Once home, Dad pumped up a handful of cool water to wash his face while each boy held a pantleg. "Tell us Daddy, was the train fun?"

"Oh yes, coming home is always fun, because you live here. The last day at the power plant a bad storm rolled across the mountains. I jumped into our Company auto, one of the new models with the cloth top and the isenglass windows, with toolboxes on the running boards. You'll see one someday. The rain was almost solid as we headed across the mountain road toward the harbor where I was ticketed on a big steamship to take me to New York.

There are no trains yet in those mountains going toward New England. Well, the dirt roads got muddier every hour, and finally we slid into the ditch! While the driver and I were trying to get the car back on the road, I kept praying that some miracle would get us to the boat before it left the pier. I prayed that if anything happened to me in the storm, you boys and Mother would be taken care of. God seemed to tell me not to worry, that He was handling the weather.

"Sure enough. Help soon arrived, in the form of a big moonshiners' truck loaded with empty barrels. It couldn't get past until they pulled us out of the ditch, then we both headed for the port where the boat had docked. The lightning and rain slowed us down. We knew that we would barely make it. As we came over the crest of the hill by the Bay, we saw the running lights of the steamship way past the flashing lighthouse a mile from the dock! My heart sank; I wondered why God had let me miss my boat by just a few minutes.

The driver and I grinned to cover our disappointment. We turned around and headed north to seek a depot on a railroad leading to New York. That made me late getting home, boys . . . But that's not all.

When I reached Grand Central the newsboys were shouting, 'Steamship lost at sea. ALL drowned! I bought a *Times*; and there on the front page was a picture of *my ship!* It had mysteriously blown up just 20 minutes out of the harbor." Dad swallowed hard. "You have your father today because God pushed his auto into the ditch! God doesn't have to explain his miracle or tell us why or how He does them. He loves us too much to discuss the details! . . . Let me hug you all again . . . it's so good to be home! Now take my hands and let's all say together, "The Lord is my shepherd ... He leadeth me ... Thank you, Master.''

MIRACLE 9

Head of the House

"Hear, my sons, the instructions of a father; and attend to know understanding, for I give you good doctrine." Prov. 4:1, 2

Boys and woodsheds have had much in common throughout New England's history. The influence of each on the other have been recorded on canvas, in stories, and through cartoons. A woodshed was just as essential as a bathtub since both removed stains from the character. And what boy wasn't a character at some time? Certainly the Eby boys were no exception.

Mother kept saying that it was a miracle they didn't drown, didn't fall out of trees, didn't break ankles running across stoney fields, or didn't get poison ivy picking blackberries down by the swamp (which was off-limits).

But father's analysis was a bit different. His Swiss-German blood would surface when he interpreted "a departure from proper deportment" as being "an intentional apostasy from the straight and narrow!" He explained that it hurt him deeply to discipline the children, but that it was his responsibility as a father who loved them.

This logic was accepted as ridiculous by the boys who would be told to go down to the water's edge where the willows grew, and cut a suitable branch for a whip. Even the smallest shoots they could find smarted real bad when Dad swatted their bare legs and sternly advised against future misconduct!

Unless it was a terrible crime requiring isolation in the bedroom during dinner, Dad would hold the sobbing boy till good sense returned, then tell him to run and correct the discovered wrong! When the punishment was over, it was remarkable how soon Dad could forgive and forget . . . a lot sooner than the boys could, they discovered!

Somehow, but slowly, the lesson began to sink in that it was only fair for Dad to insist on their good behavior in return for his working so hard all day to provide whatever they needed. Even at Sunday School the Bible said the same thing: children were to obey their parents because Jesus loved them all and promised them longer lives if they did so. He had made the father head of the home, and the mother his helpmate. It did sound like a real smart arrangement . . . except when there were fresh cookies in the jar. And then it took raw courage to obey the rules about "hands off."

One July day father dropped a bombshell. He announced that the time had come to move into town! Robert was already five years old and must start "school" (another word for "Jail" where children had to sit in chairs and answer questions, and couldn't dig worms or collect crayfish from under wet rocks. Worse yet, Richard would be in the same classroom and never would they be be able to keep from giggling when they waved at each other behind the teacher's back).

Richard had often wondered as an 8-year-old how he had escaped school, unaware that for 3 years the school doctor had certified him as being too underdeveloped to enter first grade. He had assumed he was "born free" to live at the Lake: that was where he felt at home. Besides his Mom and Dad had taught him all he needed to know, hadn't they?

Despite all objections it became obvious that Dad was serious. He had been praying for a house near enough to a school for Richard to walk there, on sidewalks too. It had to be a bargain since he had very little money left after raising the family on his modest salary. (The Company gave him $1.00 and a thankyou note for each invention, but that "generous" bonus went into the boys "college fund")

"Miracle home in the city," 2 blocks from school, and a bargain at $8000.

Dad exclaimed, "Today it has happened once again—another answer to prayer! A sturdy home near Dawes School has just been put up for sale to settle an estate in a hurry—at half its value—including a barn and garden—on a main street with sidewalks! My banker friend from church can arrange the loan, and we will be moved in before school opens the Tuesday after Labor Day!"

Bewildered, the boys wondered why Mom and Dad bowed their heads and said "Thankyou, thankyou" while they were crying. (Grownups do such weird things!) Mother was whispering, "It's another miracle; just when we needed it. YOU have prepared a place for us again: One of your mansions . . ." Dad said something about ". . . from everlasting to everlasting Thou art God . . ." and then he took their hands and led them up the stairs past their "lightning window." With a kiss he tucked them into bed. His glasses were all wet, but he seemed to be seeing all right, in fact very clearly this particular night!

MIRACLE 10

Not By Might

"Avenge not yourselves, beloved, but give place unto the wrath of God; for it is written, Vengeance belongeth unto Me, I will recompense, saith the Lord." Romans 12:19

Dawes School and Miss Denny were synonymous. She looked like a principal and proved it. Her white hair was a fitting crown for the air of dignity and discipline which her erect posture and firm step displayed as she checked out her teachers and their classrooms each morning. She was carved for the role: firm, fair and fearless. No child could guess how long she had ruled at Dawes: probably forever. She loved children—when they loved their school!

Clutching their first sack lunch, the scared boys said goodbye to Mother and turned to enter the school door. They were here to begin their new lives behind desks, but it would be hard to settle down after yesterday's last trip to the Lake for a Labor Day outing. They had said a tearful goodbye to the frogs and bluegills and crayfish under "their" dock, and helped Dad pick the Burpee peas and summer squash before waving goodbye to the quiet garden at Castle Windy. Without looking back Dad had taken their hands and started the hike (no Whoa-Dick anymore) down Hancock Road to the streetcar station and toward a life of school rooms.

It was quite another world in that post-war city where so many families were trying to "put it together again." Richard was the first to find this out. Even before recess the first-grade strangers began sizing each other up. City kids found this procedure both expedient and exciting—it established a pecking order! Robert had easily blended in with the others of his own size and age, but Richard was peculiar: he looked older but he was a runt. Besides, he was always first to raise his hand to answer the teacher's questions that morning—obviously trying to be a big-shot. He even knew the pledge of allegiance and could write the alphabet! Whispers spread: "What a puny guy—let's get rid of him and quick!"

By recess the plans had jelled: when Miss Denny wasn't looking down from her second floor window they would form a circle on the schoolyard and push Richard into the center along with Joe.

Joe had proved his prowess in kindergarten already; his Italian father wanted him to be the best boxer in the "Wap district" down by the railroad yard behind the G.E. buildings. And Joe had learned his lessons well: hit first, aim for the eyes, and duck away.

It was no contest. Richard had never seen a fist fight before, let alone understand its purpose. This first recess was bewildering anyway; school had just started and already the teacher had let them out! And now he was being honored by his roommates (probably because of his older age) by being selected at the center of a circle of admirers!

He wasn't even looking when it hit! A blinding blow in the eye then one on the bridge of his nose. Blood squirted and the air seemed filled with ringing bells. The sun went out for several minutes. No pain yet. Then it arrived; a seering throbbing torture in his head punctuated with jabbing kicks in the ribs. "Get up, you sissy." "You're too old to fight." "You don't know nuthin'. . . ."

And then they were gone and Miss Denny was standing there, grimfaced. She had feared this very thing—a delicate-built gentle boy thrown among city-bred children now reacting to their war-torn homelife. She phoned his mother to come get him. There would be no more school for him this first day, nor for the rest of the week.

It was quite a funny face, all colors and swollen! He had hid in his room when Dad was due to arrive from work that evening. The shame was overwhelming. What would Dad say when he learned his oldest son "got licked"? Dad was such a brave man, and now he had a sissy for a son. Tears of defeat plus tears of pain stained his pillow as his pounding fists dented the chicken feathers inside.

The door opened, and there stood Dad. Richard couldn't look. He wished he were dead already! This had to be the worst day of his life—he hated school and all those taunting kids! And then the mattress sagged and he felt Dad's hands around his head—soft and warm, but strong and comforting (now he knew how those chicks in the pail must have felt when he lifted them out and held them close). His pain eased.

In the few minutes since Mother had met him at the back door to quickly relate the day's events, Dad's mind had passed from anger and vengeance to sympathy and concern, and finally to peace and counsel. He had known that a moment must come when Richard would have to face certain facts: it was a real world out there, mostly without love. Some school children were cruel by nature. And most of them sturdier than he. There would be many lost fights, both within himself and with others. But there was hope—lots and lots of it. And there was respect and love . . . if he could merit it.

"I hear your first day at school was exciting, son," he said as though nothing was amiss. "It isn't everybody that gets top billing at his first appearance! You know, it was two years before I got a beautiful shiner like yours at school. To my first teacher I pretended that I could see my books and the blackboard, but the next teacher caught on and made me wear big thick glasses—the only ones in class! And did I get whopped! Those kids caught me in the outhouse at recess and broke my glasses into a hundred pieces. Then they blacked my eyes when I couldn't see to fight back. I believe that my pride was hurt more than my face." There was a smile in his voice when recalling past events. . . .

"Well, my Dad was the local judge, and he stood 6½ feet tall! He looked down at me and laughed for a while. Then he said, 'Eugene, you have 2 choices: you can sue them and maybe lose again; or you can love them and let them shrivel with shame. If you choose the latter, you can end up the tallest in class.' That's all he said. The next Sunday he rode with me on our plough horse to church. As he lifted me off I heard him say: 'By the way, son, did you love your enemies to death at school? 'Pears to me there are no new scars. Case dismissed, I presume?' He wasn't expecting an answer this time."

I had already forgotten my problem. Dad explained how he had decided to use his head rather than fists to outrank the classmates, even though thick glasses made

Union Baptist Church donated by Dad's grandfather for community worship where Dad rode horse to Sunday School.

study by candlelight a headache! Eventually he was made class president and valedictorian, and selected as the favorite baseball pitcher. "Just for fun I learned to play the violin to give two promising girl musicians a run for their money; by graduation they were really good after competing with me." Dad chuckled as was his custom whenever he did a favor without it being noticed! "Let's go down to supper; Mother just made a shortcake to celebrate the first school day. She thinks of the nicest things, doesn't she?" At supper Dad spent extra time asking a blessing on 'most everything!

By Monday the miracle had happened: Richard's terror had been drained away and replaced with a stubborn resolve to stick it out. The second week at Dawes went smoothly. In fact the kids acted sheepish when they glanced at his greenish eyelids during recess. "Boxer Joe" tried to pick a few more half-hearted fights, but he had lost his backers. He ended up asking Richard for help with his homework.

A second miracle was engineered by Miss Denny: she gave a third grade test to the first graders, figuring Richard alone could pass it and thus be advanced. Instead, five passed and went to "Third." Robert, still in first, became an instant hero by smuggling his crickets into class to relieve the boredom. All in all, that first year became exciting. The boys agreed that Dad had been smart after all in moving to town. He did seem to be learning fast of late!

MIRACLE 11

Black is Beautiful

"Jehovah preserveth the simple. I was brought low and He saved me." Psalms 116:6

By Christmastime each year Pontoosuc had become a glassy playground for the family, but here in town skating rinks were rare because most city lots slanted. For example, the vacant one across the street sloped sharply toward a big culvert ten feet below the street level. The boys discovered that the surface water from the adjoining 60-acre farm drained there. It took but a few days for them to figure out how to plug the big pipe under the street and produce a "lake." Sure enough: the sudden freeze that followed the next heavy rain made a perfectly good rink out of that useless lot overnight. That day's conversation naturally turned to skating. Robert asked Dad if boys had skates "in those old days."

"Oh my, yes! We Michigan farm boys practically lived on skates all winter. Besides the fun, we often had to skate across Baldwin Lake to get to our neighbors marooned by snowdrifts across the roads. Oftimes we would skate to church or school. During ice storms we could skate to the corner store for buttons and thread to make our printed summer shirts out of chickenfeed sacks.

One-room school-house in Union where Dad skated to classes on icy days in the '90's.

It made the cozy winter nights pass quickly while we hummed tunes from an old hymnal." Just then Mother brought in a pie, and all stopped to admire her work as she cut six equal wedges.

"Speaking of skating, boys, would you like to hear about my escape from death when I was about your age?"

Richard thought Dad was kidding for sure. "Did you really die, or almost?" "Thanks to God, He sent me a guardian angel just in time! It was a close call. The whole town called it a real miracle." He closed his eyes a moment. "I can well remember that cold Saturday afternoon in Union. Three of four groups of farmers around the Lake were sawing thick ice into big blocks to store in their "ice-houses" under sawdust till summertime. Strong horses were pulling the blocks out of the water and up onto stout sleds used just for carrying these heavy cakes back to their buildings. This "ice-harvesting" on weekends left wide strips of open water near the shoreline till they froze over again. Sometimes on Sundays we would set tip-ups along the edges and fish through the ice for lake trout or pickerel."

Dad took a couple of bites of pumpkin pie and continued. "I was so busy skating with my playmates that I failed to notice when my father drove his sled away. It was fast getting dark when I saw I was alone, so I took a short-cut toward home directly across the Lake. About fifty yards from that shore I suddenly dropped through an "ice-cut" into the water and went to the bottom. My heavy skates and boots acted like anchors. I struggled to get to the surface, but no use. Frantically I unlaced my boots and kicked them off. With a desperate lunge I pushed upward and hit my head on *ice*. . . . I had drifted past the hole and could not see it in the dark. My lungs were bursting so I used my last breath to yell, 'Save me, Lord, save me!' and then I passed out."

"Don't stop now, Dad. Did Jesus save you? . . . I mean how did He save you?" All eyes were riveted on the story-teller.

"Well, that is the miracle. A while later I woke up, like coming through a fog, wrapped in an old army blanket and smelling like whiskey. Rocking me gently was a thin black lady shouting over and over, 'Gawdall Mighty, Youse gotta hep this young 'un!' Between her prayers she yelled at a black boy to put more sticks on the fire. I'll never forget her screaming prayers: she truly knew that Someone Big was right there in the cabin with her." Dad stopped to "sample" another piece of his favorite pie.

"I guess you know already that we never understand just why or how our great and good Father protects us," he continued. "By some miracle there must have been an air bubble trapped under the ice, put there for me to breathe. The freezing water made my mind go unconscious, but God kept my fingers scratching forward under the ice until I reached the hole, and then He must have lifted me out and pointed me crawling toward the shore. The black boy came along just then looking for firewood and found me instead! He was so scared, he admitted later, that he simply dragged me back to the abandoned cabin where his shivering mother had taken shelter for the night. She had stripped off my mackinaw and clothing, wrapped me in her only blanket, and poured whiskey between my teeth. Believe me, that stuff is horrid: don't use it unless you drown!''

The awe-struck boys nodded vigorously. They had once come upon a "drunk" at Pontoosuc. Did he smell horrid! And looked it too! Again at school it was also horrid whenever a classmate had no lunch because his Dad was "soused" and his Mom "didn't have any money for food after he got fired." Richard would often pretend he wasn't hungry so he could share with a less fortunate friend the favorite peanut butter sandwich in his sack. Who would want booze, for goodness sake, when there

Doctor Dick   Engineer Eugene   Counsellor Cassius

On Michigan Centennial Farm 3 generations pause to discuss God's management of Eby's for nearly 200 years since leaving Switzerland.

was peanut butter instead? Whiskey? Who needed it?

Dad's story had to be interrupted long enough to finish the pie and lick the forks. Dad leaned forward and grasped a small hand on each side. He had something more to say.

"Sometimes when we are young and cold and frightened Jesus can teach us a special lesson. He had one for me that night . . . it was about the way He plans ahead so He can have the right answers ready when we are in trouble. You see, even before I was born, *He* knew I would fall through the ice, but He didn't want me to drown. He just wanted to show me how very much He loved a stupid little boy who would skate in the dark. So He arranged ahead for a poor black mother (without husband or home) to find an abandoned old cabin on the shore just a few yards from where He knew I would fall in. Then He made it extra cold so her boy would go hunting for more firewood. And He made sure I found the hole and would crawl out at the very moment we should meet." He paused for this simple wisdom to sink in.

"Jesus arranged another answer too: that black lady needed *His* help to find work. When your Grandpa came looking for me, he stopped to investigate the sparks coming from the deserted old cabin, and found me in the lady's arms, still talking to her 'Gawd.' Then he bundled us into the sleigh and galloped the horses all the way home! Can you imagine? That very day a farmer at Paw Paw had phoned "Judge Eby" (Dad's business name) looking for a "Christian colored maid" and "a young farmhand" since he had been unable to locate any help for months. The next morning my kind lady and her boy both had jobs! The farmer couldn't understand how the Judge had located help so fast!"

Dad's boyhood home in Union where he thawed out after falling through the ice cut.

"Can you see the lesson Jesus taught me? How He
turns upside-down into rightside-up? How He honors
prayers even when you're drowning? How He loves people of any color? I learned He runs an employment agency
too. The "Sunday Jesus" we worship at Church goes
home with us all week and "works all things together" for
our good. That includes frozen white boys, hungry black
boys, and even your crotchety old parents!" He smiled
and looked toward the kitchen. "Of course we mustn't
wait for God to do the dishes. Tonight you wash, and I'll
dry."

MIRACLE 12

The Influence

> "Blessed be . . . the God of all comfort: who comfort-
> eth us in all our afflictions that we may be able to
> comfort them that are in any affliction."
> I Corinthians 1:3, 4

To this day Richard can remember the ghoulish
nightmare that descended upon Pittsfield the following
winter.

The headlines called it "Influenza," although no one
dared theorize what dastardly "influence" had waved its
deathly hand across every village in the land. Medical
texts would later record it as a new "strain" of organism
not previously identified as epidemic in nature. From
pulpits the remaining harried pastors declared that Satan
was now attacking this Christian nation because Praying
Americans had won the World War under the guidance of
God and His armies, and this had made the devil angry.
No better explanation emerged; ancient recorded history
favored the conclusion that some kind of mighty struggle
for men's minds and bodies had been waged in every
generation since Eve ate forbidden fruit and then raised
Cain!

Like the dark shadow of an advancing cold front, this
epidemic fell across families from the eastern seaboard to

Pittsfield and on toward the Pacific. Our house on Holmes Road became quiet. Unshovelled snow piled into 10-foot drifts. The isolated pullets in their buried henhouse out back pecked futilely through straw for bits of remaining cracked corn. Traffic stopped. Not even horses could get through the snow. Most phone lines were down or buried. Newsboys on snowshoes tried to deliver the weekly paper and earn their 10¢ a day for cough syrup. The headlines told of thousands of bodies unburied at cemeteries where the ground was too frozen for the flu-weakened workmen to dig graves. A few months later the Berkshire Eagle reported "Flu Kills More Than Entire World War."

Mother came down first. Tired out, from tending her sick neighbors she shot a fever to 104° overnight. Dad and the boys took up a vigil at her bedside that morning, vainly trying to "force fluids" and cool her hot face with washcloths, and get her to swallow broken aspirins down her raw throat.

By night she was delirious and the boys felt "horrid" too. One vomited and the other had diarrhea. Both started to cough. Dad tucked them in their beds and prayed as never before: "Lord, I commit my family into Your care; please bring them through safely! And give *me* strength to stay on my feet and help them . . ." He hadn't told them that his chest was on fire inside and his head pounded like a piledriver. By morning they were all delirious.

During fleeting lucid moments that week Dad crawled out of bed and made rounds. He shook so hard that it was easy for him to get the mercury back down in the glass thermometer by simply holding it. In each mouth it registered over 103°. The beds were already soaked with sweat, and each boy tossed fitfully. Outside the snow kept falling silently like a muted requiem.

Later he remembered phoning Dr. Barrett and pleading for a house call. Doc begged off: "Gene, I hate to tell you this but I'm dead on my feet. We few doctors have divided up the town and assigned a section to each of us. We have to go on snowshoes pulling a toboggan-full of supplies. It's slow work, with a stop at almost every house. I'll be out your way in about four days."

When Doc came, there was little new to do, he said sadly: things looked real bad. Richard was screaming off and on with nightmares. He had seen his very first airplanes last July 4th, a whole skyfull in formation, flying over Pittsfield from Boston to Albany. Above the town a few had pealed off and done acrobatics with their screaming engines echoing across the valley. For five days now they had been dive-bombing his bed, roaring through his head and back up to the ceiling. Deliriously he grabbed his pillow and tried to hide; they still gunned him down. Several times he fell off the bed but they were down there too. Some fell in flames and hit him in the chest; then he'd cough up bloody remains.

Despite those dreadful days God and Dad were "tending His store," like a saddened Shepherd holding sick lambs. Dad said afterwards that he never doubted that his family would make it. He could not pray much though, because he was unconscious most of the time on the floor or on the divan or wherever he fell after staggering from room to room with his offerings of cold water or toast or egg. When the fevers finally subsided, it was hard to recognize one another. Dad looked skinny and old and Mom was wrinkled. The boys pants fell off their hips, and their eyes looked hollow. Through the windows they could see black wreaths hanging on almost every door up and down the street. By some miracle though none was needed at their house.

Doctor Barrett would only shake his head when asked why our family had recovered at all. Thirty years later he told "Dr. Dick" that those of his patients who had survived that epidemic all had something in common: they had acted like they knew they would live even while they were delirious! Like Dad, several of them had continued to give nursing care to others in their homes without apparently being conscious. Afterwards they could not remember what they did. Dr. Barrett admitted that something called 'faith' seemed to be the miracle that made the difference. "You know, Dick, we doctors have very little to offer in serious diseases. Since I've known your Dad, I'm inclined to believe him. He claims that whenever someone gets well it is because God has plans for using him to help another; when someone dies, His work is done. We don't learn that in college, but we don't learn a lot of things in classrooms! He has me almost persuaded that God knows what He's doing even when we don't understand at all. . . ."

MIRACLE 13

School Work and Buckshot

"And David said moreover, The Lord that delivered
me out of the paw of the lion, and out of the paw of
the bear, He will deliver me out of the hand of this
Philistine. And Saul said unto David, Go, and the
Lord be with thee." I Samuel 17:37

Junior High was three years of fun. The teachers
"poured it on" and the class competed for "A's." It
became a contest to outwit the teachers by studying a
lesson ahead. They became frustrated standing up in front
and finding little new to teach that day. Miss Denny
wondered what was going on in "that class of eighth
graders" (but she was really responsible). When she had
moved those five first-graders to third grade years ago,
and the next year jumped them to fifth, she had produced
five little zealots determined to set records. Then it became
infectious: forty of their classmates caught the spirit and
records fell.

Realizing that a college education in the "twenties"
was for most youngsters a futile dream, Miss Denny had
set up a voluntary "High School Preparatory Program" so
her pupils could advance that far at least toward their
goals. Dick (as he was now called) and his friend Henry
were the ring-leaders in talking their class into signing up.

That meant Latin, French, advanced algebra, rhetoric and instrumental music, in addition to the usual Junior high subjects. Of course, the fringe benefits of athletic activities and woodworking, and sewing classes for girls, continued as usual. However, each teacher assigned an hour of homework per subject per night: that was a weighty problem right off the bat!

So Henry and Dick organized the class. On a rotation basis four classmates were assigned to do the homework on each of the five subjects each night. Each "studier" reported the next morning the highlights of the day's upcoming lessons. Recess provided time for filling in details! It worked better than expected. Only the teachers were dubious: they couldn't figure out how this particular class got "100's" on tests without cheating. In fact, Miss Denny hesitated to announce at their graduation from Junior High the following year that all but three students had averaged above "90" for their full three years. She felt that other Junior High principals in town would complain that she had lowered the standards at Dawes!

If she could have looked into the future her heart would have leaped instead. From her "star class" of assorted kinds of kids she would see Henry, a Lever Bros. vicepresident; Dick, a College President and physician; Rita, a Boston Conservatory artist; Fred, a large corporation lawyer; Paul, the leading Hollywood composer; Dennis, an international importer; and Vera, a noted artist in oils. The list would include bankers, merchants, musicians, and an author or two, topped with the highest compliment of all: several teachers, from grade school levels through college professors! God had honored her commitment to hard work and long suffering, and documented it in the Book of Good Works. It surely includes her name today now that she rests in unaccustomed peace awaiting her day before the Greatest Teacher of them all!

Besides the "miracle" of making schoolwork into fun, the system had developed fringe benefits, such as *freed time* to grow up doing what came *happily*. For Dick it meant time for roaming the mountainsides where his nature friends abounded, and for tooting his French horn in any band or orchestra that needed one. Both hobbies paid off: one in better muscles and the other in better sounds. Hiking offered solitude for unleashing frustrations born of his physical limitations and discomforts, whereas music forced him to suppress his innate timidity and fear of bigger people. (He would never quite win either battle, but he could come close to victory by asking his Lord to lend a hand.)

We practice "A Mighty Fortress" under the favorite pictures in the colonial living room.

It was while hiking in early October with his pal Wilbur along Roaring Brook that he had another miracle. Luscious blackberries were in season and the upper sides of the steep banks were overhung with fruitladen bushes interspersed with brush and goldenrod. The Fall air and the upstream effort of "stonehopping" created an instant need for such nourishment.

On hands and knees Dick started his crawl up the gulley wall and pulled himself halfway over the loose dirt edge covered with brush. The woodsey silence was suddenly shattered! A shotgun roared, only a few feet from his face. A shower of punctured red and yellow leaves fell around his head with a spray of blackberry juice adding a bloody color to his sweaty shirt. Reflexly he released his hold on the exposed roots and fell backwards down the bank. Wilbur stood shock-frozen, his tongue trying to yell to the unseen hunter that had killed his pal! (If a camera could have caught the scene, it would have looked posed.)

Dick recovered first and yelled: "Stay down, Wilbur! He thinks we're rabbits or a deer." His warning was not necessary. They could hear someone running away through the dry twigs and brush, more scared than they were, and not about to be found near a "dead man." Wilbur came running, blanched with fear. Then they laughed a hysterical giggle at first, and finally a full rush of hearty relief. What a lousy shot! How could that guy expect to hit a rabbit if he couldn't hit a boy! He sure ruined that blackberry bush! . . .

"But how come you didn't get hit in the face, Dick? You must have been born lucky or somethin', that's all I can say!" exclaimed a bewildered Wilbur. En route home through the lowland meadows they exchanged small-talk only. There are times when growing boys must retreat within their minds to do a mental taffy-pull, tugging a sticky problem back and forth till it makes sense and takes form. Being shot at, and being missed, is a bit of a jolt to any fourteen-year-old, or his friend. Miracles were becoming mighty personal things to Dick, so he held his growing collection of thoughts close to his heart. (Someday, at the right time, he would tell about them.) Wilbur, on the other hand, wasn't sure there were such things; neither could he tell himself today that there weren't. . . . Best avoid the subject and chew a blade of timothy; besides, let's figure out why little grasshoppers are green and big ones are brown. Dick should know, he was usually fooling around with creepy things anyway!

MIRACLE 14

Arise and Be Healed

"Until now you have not asked for anything in My Name; ask and you shall receive, so that your happiness may be complete" John 16:24

Summer boys' camps were a relatively new idea in the twenties. They were being spawned out of the desperate needs of crowded city dwellers to "get away from it all." Children living at the bottoms of canyon walls between tenement fire escapes ganged up on anyone handy—mostly on their weary parents at first, then each other, then society. If a tree really grew in Brooklyn, few had seen it! Garbage-littered sidewalks crept outward from city centers to engulf the original greenery which had made America beautiful when people first arrived.

God began to move across the face of society, first touching the sensitive souls in His churches, then other organizations established to help fellowmen. The Berkshire Hills had been seemingly spared from over-population in order to offer an ideal spot for "big-city kids" to stand on green grass and see a white cloud of changing patterns float across a blue sky. With this new vision the Pittsfield YMCA took its few pennies from the bank and opened Camp Sumner on the shores of Pontoosuc Lake. How many young lives were affected by this program through the following years is somewhere recorded in a Heavenly Book. It affected Dick and Bob.

"There's a phone call for you, Richard," Mother announced as he walked through the back door. Richard, still lost in thought, didn't react. In a month he would graduate from Junior High and there was so much to do during "vacation." Horn lessons, Sunday School duties, garden and lawn chores, library visits, picking blueberries to sell to earn bike money, and hopefully fishing and hiking in between.

"Richard!!! You are to call Mr. Besserer at the YMCA . . . something about a Camp." His mind sat upright! Camp? The one thing he had feared was that Mom would find out about Camp Sumner, and would want him to go. "Oh no . . . I'm not going to be made out a fool and a weakling again, *not again*," he thought angrily. He pretended to adjust the rubberbands that held the braces on his crooked teeth. (The dentist said his jaws were too small for the size of his teeth but by pulling out a front one and "forcing the bite" it should "help his face.") The subtle ridicule at school among classmates was bad enough. No way was he going to attend camp among *strange* boys! He knew he was timid, and weak, and shy—compared with others his age. And he feared what Mr. Besserer, the Camp Director, had in mind for him . . . to *make him over* into a man . . . Besserer, a human dynamo with three little daughters when he had wanted a son . . . Besserer, who had taken a shine to an industrious little bow-maker in the beginner's archery class at the "Y." Oh, well . . .

He lifted the earpiece: "Number, Paahl-ease." "6025-ring 2." . . . "Thah-ank You."

He hated telephones ever since that first day at Castle

Windy when the man had bored a hole for a wire and screwed a funny box on the wall. Mom had said to clean up the sawdust but had said nothing about turning the crank and listening at the black handle with the little holes in the end. A tinny voice had screamed into his ear: "You little kid, get off the line, and never use this phone again! Don't you know anything? Someone might need it for an emergency." He would never enjoy phoning again.

. . ."Besserer speaking. . . . Oh, Dick, my boy. Great news. I spoke to your mother and she says it's alright to sign you up for Tent Four. There'll be 7 other boys all from New York except the one from Amherst—his Dad is Professor of Botany there. And more good news . . . the "Y" Directors gave me permission to put you in charge of Nature Study and Museum Development on weekdays, and Camp Devotions on Sundays. You can lead singing and play your horn. How does that sound? You can attend Camp free, they tell me."

Inside Dick died. "Thank you, sir. I will discuss it with my parents first. I had other plans, you know." Yes, Besserer knew; however, he wanted his Directors to see what he could do with a timid boy under his guidance that summer. Dick would be his "project" if only he could get him to Camp. "Train up a child in the way he should go, and when he is old, he shall not depart from it!"

That phone call was to be a pivotal point in his life; 50 years later "Dr. Dick" would realize this. He would then know that victories are won by losing battles; that God's strength is made perfect in weakness; that unless a seed falls in the ground and dies, it can not live; that "For Thy sake we are killed all day long; we are accounted as sheep for the slaughter—nay, in all things we are more than conquerors." But it didn't seem right then.

He lost his first real contest of wills that evening in the living room. He had mounted every argument against going to Camp—even to claiming he would surely drown during the first compulsory swimming contest from the "Y" dock out to the floating platform where the trained horse did its diving act every Saturday.

But Mom and Dad had remained firm: he *must* learn to mix with other boys . . . *forget* the braces, *forget* the weak back and legs, *forget* the fear of failure! *Win* with confidence at whatever you *can* do! *Share* with the city lads the beautiful things you have learned these years in God's country! *Teach* them about flowers and trees and bugs. *"Tell* them God loves you, and therefore He must also love them: maybe they don't know that!"

"Tell you what: Robert can go along too if he will agree to leave his magnets and coils and homemade transformers that long!" Dick surrendered with that "carrot."

Corner of Nature Museum at Camp Sumner showing Richard's "specimens in jars," match-up board, and terrarium.

Bob was big; he could run interference when called on. Somehow the summer would pass. After all, it was one way of getting time with his first love, Pontoosuc.

Director Besserer ran the Camp like a benevolent general with each youthful "aide" strutting his stuff before his 7 little charges. At daybreak they would roll out of the canvas bunks, head for the outhouse, assemble around the flagpole for devotions and instructions, then race to messhall. Then back to clean the tent, and prepare for "Projects." Nature Study was always the favorite—it meant hikes into the hills or around the Lake—and "Eby" was "alright"—he acted like a kid himself.

Camp life went smoothly until the first big accident. Dick had led 21 excited butterfly-chasers that day along the brook where the largest mustard and goldenrod and Queen Ann's Lace grew. Swarms of fritillaries and swallowtails with occasional monarchs and mourning cloaks vied for sweet nectar, fluttering daintily around each bloom. The boys took off in all directions shouting as they spotted a special "beauty." Benny, the professor's son from Amherst College, the smartest of the group, had run ahead up the stream bed where the butterflies would be less disturbed. What Dick did not know was that Benny had a cyanide jar in his pocket "borrowed" from his Dad's laboratory for killing insects instantly. A sudden cry of pain signalled trouble! Dick arrived first. Benny was sprawled where he had slipped on a wet stone. His shorts were dripping blood. Between white knuckles he was trying to hold a huge gash together on his right thigh. "What in the world happened, Benny?" gasped Dick. A frightened boy sobbed back: "I fell right on the bottle and it broke into my leg. . . . It's POISON! Will I die? . . . Help me!"

There was no time to answer. Off came the shorts with its pocket full of broken glass and cyanide crystals imbedded in plasterparis. Dick had made such bottles for his own use at home—and knew that cyanide in the body fluids was fatal. He stripped off his own shirt for a tourniquet and pulled the wound tight enough to stop the pumping blood. Already Benny was pallid. With five boys on each side forming a living stretcher under Benny's shocky body, they quickly headed back to camp. Dick sent the swiftest boy running ahead to summon an ambulance from town. A solemn-faced ring of campers was waiting for them twenty minutes later when the procession arrived. Besserer took over the first aid till a white Reo with the big red cross on its hood roared up from the highway.

Among the campers the word had spread fast that Benny was "a goner." The doctor on the ambulance had blanched when he heard "cyanide," and without realizing that he was overheard he told the driver to *step on it.* "He probably can't last till we get him to surgery. . . . Deep cut. . . . Cyanide, you know."

Richard's "Tent Four Gang" at Camp Sumner
"Cyanide Boy"—back row, left.

Dick disappeared down the lane into a clump of black birch trees where someone had left an old bench. He was crushed. Surely he would be expelled from camp now. As a "tent leader" and "nature director" he was responsible for the lives of his children. The amount of cyanide in that jar could kill a hundred boys in seconds. How could he face Benny's family at the funeral? How could he face Besserer? How could he explain to his parents who trusted him to do right?

It was the first time he had ever faced great personal tragedy alone, and the first time he had no one but Jesus to talk to. He had never had to pray for anything really important: Dad and Mom did that. He didn't know whether he even dared ask Jesus to save Benny from death; that was a huge order for a youngster to request! At Church only the minister prayed for healing, and then only after the doctors had given up. Anyway, it was worth a try to ask Him. . . . The Bible said "Ask and you will receive."

"Please, Jesus, Benny needs help real bad. Don't let him die. And don't forget to help his Dad and Mom. Please . . . please help him get well . . . please."

Word finally came the next morning from the hospital. For some "unexplained" reason Benny had come out of shock following the emergency surgery to cut away the dying muscle tissue; he was "stabilized." His father arrived at Camp by noon to thank Mr. Besserer and the "Young Nature Leader" for saving his boy with such quick first aid. He apologized to the circle of anxious faces around him for the "indiscretion" of his son in smuggling a cyanide bug bottle into camp. If Sumner officials would let his boy back next year, Benny would return to show them "his miracle scar"!

It was remarkable what a large attendance Richard had all week at vespers. No boy could forget Benny, and the campfire flickered on little faces whose thoughts had suddenly grown wiser. Besserer invoked a heavenly benediction upon them "and upon our campmate in the Hospital whom you are healing so miraculously!" And the stars seemed to shine unusually bright over Tent 4 with its empty bunk. God was healing Benny because someone believed His promise!

MIRACLE 15

Master, the Tempest

"And there arose a great storm of wind, and the waves beat into the ship, so that it was now full."
Mark 4:37

"This is the Limit!" Whenever we heard Dad make this clarion announcement, it meant we had arrived at Lake Champlain, and our two-week vacation had started! Every year he planned ahead to get there, and about half the time he made it. This was a special year for him because Bob was back from Wheaton, Dick was here from Los Angeles and with him was Maybelle, his fiancée from Chicago. Kid sister Helen and May could have "girl talk" for hours!

About nine years ago Dad had first rented this old cottage on Long Point, at North Ferrisburg, Vermont, sight unseen from a newspaper ad. Described was a two-storey, 4-bedroom summer place at the end of the two-track trail along a small peninsula jutting into the "pickerel waters." This ad was bait enough for a fish-happy engineer and his True-Temper rod with its polished South Bend reel. This year the Limit ("the end of the road") was again available, and here we were!

Although Dad's vision was dimmed by cataracts, it in no way dimmed his enthusiasm to "get going." The 142-

Long Point "lunkers." Helen has 5 fishes, needs 7 loaves?

mile drive from Pittsfield, north through the Green Mountains along narrow curvaceous strips of macadam, called for a hearty Bar-B-Q on the familiar rock ledge overhanging the water then a good night's sleep after prayertime in the moonlight. "We thank and praise you, Father, for our safe trip today! Let the words of our mouths and the meditations of our hearts be acceptable in Thy sight during our vacation. In this beautiful place let us grow in Thy grace and wisdom. We are so happy to have Dick, and Bob, and Maybelle here with Mother, Helen and me. Draw us ever closer together in Thee. And give us Thy peace! Amen."

Hardly was the sun up when the breakfasted "gang" was renting a rowboat with an "outboard." This new-fangled luxury was terribly expensive—something like a dollar-a-day—but Dad was "splurging" this summer. (It would likely be the last vacation the whole family would spend together now that both Dick and Bob were in colleges out west.) While the men practiced pulling the rope starter and pumping the choke till they had the hang of it, the girls bought them a container of nightcrawlers and two flashy bass lures. Finally, the gear was checked. Mom and Helen planned to stay home to finish the unpacking so they waved goodbye to the fishermen, rapidly disappearing over the smooth water toward the mouth of Little Otter Creek.

It would prove a day to be remembered! Blue sky, peanut butter sandwiches, and hungry bass attacking spoons and worms. Happy talk, rekindled memories, exciting philosophy. The joys of togetherness always reached these new peaks out on the water in a gently rocking row boat!

By 1 PM it was time to head for the Limit with the string of fish for supper, so Dad started the motor and away we went. A gusting ripple was seen approaching us from the distant peninsula, apparently running ahead of a dark cloud over the hill. Within 100 yards of the Point, the cloud suddenly dropped down to the water as though aiming at the small boat. Dad had been crouched in the stern admiring his new tackle box filled with well-worn lures when he felt the boat lurch; he looked up in time to see a wall of water come aboard. In seconds the lake around us was a maelstrom under the blackened sky.

"Children, we're going to sink," Dad shouted, "Boys, grab Maybelle, I'll try to make it on my own! Grab that floating oar over there! Dear God, we need Your help, and please. . . ." His head disappeared under a whitetopped wave. Maybelle screamed. She couldn't swim any more than a dog-paddle, much less stay afloat in wet clothes in these waves. Both Bob and I grabbed for her as she went under, dragging us below another monstrous breaker. Then the rain came—in bucketsful—angry, sinister, blinding; overhead a tongue of lightning struck at some floating debris.

Maybelle surfaced first, still screaming for help. Then we shot upward from below her, and saw Dad's head emerge through a chopping whitecap, his glasses miraculously still in place but of no value when wet.

"Dad, over here . . . shore's this way," Bob blurted. "Swim *into* the waves. . . ." They both disappeared again as I poked the oar under May's arms before the next wave hit. The off-shore gale had now re-doubled over our heads. I remember being sure we would drown; none of us could possibly swim to shore against those towering waves! With my mouth full of water: I could only *think* a prayer "Please, Jesus, save Dad and May. And help Bob, too!" I knew I would drown. Yet I felt suddenly quite peaceful to know my fate so quickly, as long as the others could survive.

All this time God was watching satan's attack, and listening: I know it now. At this selected moment of my final gasp for air He acted! The overturned boat was coming *at me*, and May and Bob were already halfway to the rocks where the breakers were now leaping up at the slippery stones. Blinded Dad was close behind them, riding a wave in the *right* direction! Whereas a moment before, no one had been on the raindrenched Point, now it was swarming with sopping campers wading out to grab us!

Back at the Limit we soon lay wrapped in blankets, looking like blue tuna shivering in sacks. Between chattering teeth, each survivor was talking to his Savior in his own way. No one could understand why the edge of that angry cloud had suddenly reversed direction *toward* shore while the main storm raced on across the Lake. Nor was it reasonable that the heavy outboard motor had become unscrewed, chain and all, from the overturned boat which then floated back to the surface just when Dad had groped blindly to grasp the gunwale. We learned that no one on shore had heard our screams, but a lonely lady had felt a "sudden urge" to walk out into the pelting rain. When she saw us she screamed—and everybody had heard her!

The next day we were feeling fine when the curious campers collected on the front porch to hear our story. Dad told them how thankful we were to God. He invited everyone to join with us Sunday at the Crossroads Chapel up the hill and hear about God's power over Waves. If everyone would bring a potluck dish, he suggested, we all could have a campers' picnic in the Sunday School room afterwards!

The visiting pastor was amazed at the overflow congregation that morning. It was obvious that most of the visitors weren't "church people"; they didn't know the hymns, and couldn't locate the Book of Mark in the pew Bible. Funny, too. He had felt led to preach from the fourth chapter about Jesus' disappointment over the lack of faith of the disciples when they were in rough waters! He wondered if God had maneuvered the sudden "squall" yesterday so it would hit across Long Point and lead those wayward city-folk to come to church. Who would know for sure? At least it had brought a French Horn player from Los Angeles to render a solo during the offering! "We are favored this morning to hear an old favorite— "Master, the Tempest is Raging". . . . Miss Orth from Chicago will accompany our camper friend. Incidentally, we are glad that they are such excellent swimmers. . . . I hear they rode out the storm that would have drowned most city folks!"

According to God's Word no miracle was ever performed without good reason. This past week was no exception. Jesus had planned to use it for *His* purposes.

Although Dad had lost his lifetime collection of treasured lures, he was given a deeper vision of his Lord's protecting love to compensate for his dimming eyesight. Besides, his loss permitted a host of friends to enjoy the blessings of giving him some more tackle every Christmas. Maybelle's new terror of boats and water needed release: so The Comforter led an up-Lake cabin cruiser into the harbor two days later where the skipper would learn about the near-drowning incident from the storekeeper. Without knowing why, he walked down the path, and invited "the City-girl" (and all of us) to go out in his large boat around the "scarey" Point. It worked! Ever after she was an avid boater.

When Bob and I looked back upon that fright-filled day, we realized anew how helpless are the "principalities and powers" of the air if we let the Master still the waves of our lives! Mother and sister Helen had another blessing: they discovered that their faith in Jesus' protective power permits Him to act *for them* even when they are unaware of a crisis. And God's remote Crossroads Chapel had an unexpected blessing: an opportunity that weekend to touch the lives of several campers who had least expected to intercept the Man of Galilee on their vacation! Everyone had received some measure of living water in exchange for the raging water!

En route home a week later, Dad spoke for us all in his going-home prayer: "We praise you, Father, for this wonderful time together as a family. Let us be worthy of your goodness to us. And make us ready for whatever You have in store for us next!" Bob and I exchanged glances which meant, "Yes, Lord, just what is next?"

MIRACLE 16

Six Pots of Power

"The Lord is my strength and my shield; my heart trusted in Him and I am helped; therefore my heart greatly rejoices; and with my song will I praise Him."
Psalm 28:7

There is a time and a season for all things, and Dad's life was no exception. The G.E. Company's policy on retirement was inflexible no matter how critically a program would be affected by the rule; and 1948 marked the end of the alloted 40 years of employment for him. It was to be a time of celebration and accolades, tempered by the necessary rupture of long established routines and friendships.

For his family the occasion of his "testimonial banquet" would be as climactic as had been for him the emptying of his oaken desk drawers in "Building 42." So many memories fought for his final attention! With his one good operated eye he could now read his old carefully pencilled notes. After these years they had gathered more significance while America the Beautiful was growing technical muscles from sea to shining sea. Dad had been an important, though unheralded, wheel in this march of progress. He could alway see God's hand at work, but

Dad's "Retirement Reel" and "King Tut's Porcelain Lamp."

consistently refused to take any credit for his own handiwork.

From among the papers he left behind was omitted a great story. Fortunately he had told it to Bob and me as it had developed during our High School days. To my knowledge it has never been publicly told. We treasured it then, as I do now, as a miracle of God's preparation for the needs of His creation—mankind. And Dad was a part of that divinely arranged plan beautifully executed by the Master's Mind over so many centuries. This is the way it unfolded.

I can now quote from Dad's retirement speech handwritten by him two decades ago:

> "... Perhaps the best I can do (tonight) is to reminisce a little ... My professional career almost from the start has been intimately connected with High Voltage Bushings as YOU well know! Fortunately, no one ever assigned my name to any one type; in fact, there were just too many members of my bushing family for that. However, I had a very early intimation that somehow Bushings & I were to become CLOSELY RELATED. ..."

His modesty precluded reference to his having been chosen only two years after graduation as the electrical engineer to head a new so-called "High Voltage Bushing Division." In 1908 the Company's president and genius, Dr. Charles Steinmetz, had predicted to Dad that America's future would depend upon vast voltages of electrical energy, but that the lack of proper insulators (called bushings) stood in the way. "Mr. Eby, someone in America will be found with enough inventive genius to commit himself to this unsolved task! I think I have found that man." Thus, Dad and bushings became "closely related," and mankind around the earth would someday experience the impact!

Dad could not know what God foresaw, but he never wavered from the belief that the days and nights he spent as a frustrated electrical pioneer were for a purpose. Perhaps only Mother and her boys sensed his human agony of defeat as invention after invention lay thwarted on the drawing boards for want of *one little item*: some type of porcelain which would withstand the multi-millions of electrical volts such as were loosed somewhere every day by lightning storms upon substations and cross-country high tension lines! Downtown in the unique "lightning lab" where his colleagues were bombarding bushings made of every known porcelain using *man-made* thunder-bolts, the bushings had exploded—along with their daily hopes for a final breakthrough.

I can remember one particular Saturday morning that year as Dad was eating his favorite blueberry pancakes with a "dash of country bacon grease." He seemed un-usually relaxed after a long night at his study desk in the end of his bedroom. We knew better than to start a con-versation when we could sense Dad's eagerness to impart a pearl. In the midst of the third pancake, he lay down his fork, and the crow's-foot above his cheek moved up a bit as he smiled.

"Boys, and you too, Mother," he began, "I want to share something unusual. I am still not sure what it really means." He turned a moment to admire his beloved "Honey Girl" (as four-year-old Helen had nicknamed herself already), busily wrestling with the age-old problem of getting her doll ready for its morning bath. "I finally told God last night that I was ready to give up, along with my whole staff of engineers, mechanics, test operators, chemists, and porcelain specialists! We are totally exhausted emotionally from the frustrating years of failures both here at Pittsfield and at Schenectady; even at Lynn and Pittsburg! I simply told Him that He would have to show us an answer or let the world go along with-out the blessings of His great electrical power being harnessed for His children's use. Then I fell asleep."

He sensed our impatient curiosity: "I can see you want to know His answer. Well, it's confusing. My Bible this morning fell open to an old familiar story in John, the second chapter; one I should know by heart! Something forced me to re-read it—about how Jesus changed water to wine. God started talking directly into my mind: He said quite clearly, "Know ye not that I have spoken through my Word? Did I not use 6 pots? Big ones? Was it not My power that changed the water? He that hath ears, let him hear, saith the Lord!" Dad's eyes glazed in thought as I watched his face. My heart pounded: *God* Himself had talked to *Dad* . . . *right upstairs* . . . *this morning*!

"I prayed for an interpretation," he continued. "I think it obvious what He was saying, but it would only make sense to a *Christian* engineer. Those "stone" waterpots were unusually large—up to 25 gallon capacity— probably special for that large a wedding party. To an engineer that means that the stone-like pottery was super strong. That's the first clue. There were six—not four or seven—pots. Six is the number of man, in the Scriptures. Another clue perhaps? And what about the chemistry of changing water to alcohol? It would take millions of volts to re-arrange the molecules, we are told. And the pots withstood all that power from Jesus's spoken word! It must have been like bombs going off inside those pots! I'll admit that I had never considered that part of the miracle before. It was like the power of a mustard seed moving mountains—it's known in Scripture as the Faith *of* God."

Bob and I sat silent. This was "heavy stuff" especially for breakfast. Later that afternoon as we three sat fishing and chewing slices from a cylinder of bologna, I asked Dad what he planned to do about his message from God. He answered with a question.

"What would *you* do with a big staff of tired discouraged employees? Probably what I'm planning: Monday I will declare a month's holiday and close down the Division while everyone rests. When they return we will expect an answer! God says it will be pottery, man-made and virtually blast-proof. I have no idea where to find it, but He does! By the way, your bobber has disappeared; at least we know where to find the fish today. . . ."

I knew that I was fishing with a man of God that day. There's always something instinctively special in the presence of a King's son. To me, even now, it feels like tremendous power about to explode. I did not doubt the miracle of Dad's message from Jesus; the world had to get it through someone—why not him? Now it was a simple matter of waiting for the next miracle—we both knew it must happen.

MIRACLE 17

Out of Egypt

"Marvel not at this, for the hour is coming in which all that are in the graves shall hear his voice." John 5:28

As I finish this "high voltage" story, I am reminded of a current radio commercial in Southern California; wherein the loquacious realtor concludes his pitch by warning, "If you list your house with us be prepared to move . . . fast!" That script writer must have known about the methods of Him who owns all the earth's real estate. When the Great Planner has His men all in a row, He moves *fast* too!

Rapidly a month passed and Dad's Division was back to work. Lunch-breaks became story-swapping hours as the dozens of his staff compared their vacation trips. One by one Dad casually queried his staff about any unusual events that they could recall. Surely God had done by now whatever He had in mind. Yet nothing seemed to reveal it. So Dad retraced his steps again and again. The crisis was growing nearer daily.

A White House wire arrived from President Hoover urging Dad to schedule an immediate conference regarding his huge hydro-electric project out west called Boulder Dam. The cement was soon being poured for the footings and the penstocks, and the huge transformers would soon arrive in Nevada from Pittsfield to await rewelding (after being sawed in half to permit passage through the narrow-gauge tunnels leading to the dam-site). The world's greatest dam would be useless as a power source, he pointedly noted, unless Eby solved the bushing problem—right now! Dad knew that his friend, Herbert, was dead serious. Produce, or else . . .

Dad called his Schenectady office. He must talk to his no. 1 porcelain man, Mr. Cermak, just back from overseas last week. Perhaps someone in that department had found an answer. "Is that you, Cermak? . . . Good to hear your voice and glad you're back safe. Where'd you go this time?"

"Hello, Gene! I've been wanting to call you but I had to get the plant opened and running again after your enforced shut-down. . . . Had a great time! Saw France, Rome, stopped at Greece, and stayed over two days in Egypt. Got off the boat and heard the hawker selling a camel ride to that newly opened tomb—King something— 'Tut for short. For a quarter he bounced me across the desert on that smelly beast. Say, that tomb is really something. I bribed the guard with another quarter to let me palm a souvenir, and he jumped at the chance. You must go there someday. . . . Nothin' new here on that bushing order. I hear Hoover's got his engineer's blood boiling!"

Into the night hours something kept "bugging" Dad: *God* would surely not have let him down. Pottery . . . made-made . . . ancient . . . near East . . . water jug. Like a bolt of the very lightning he was trying to control, a mental picture suddenly focused in his mind! Could it be . . . ?

"So sorry, Cermak, to phone you back at 4 A.M.! Shake off the cobwebs and try to make sense of what I am going to ask you. You said you visited a tomb—Tut's? What was the souvenir you stole when the guard looked away?"

"Now look, Gene, you wouldn't be about to get me in trouble, would you, for a measley piece of pottery?" His sleepy voice belied his surprise over being questioned. "You know, that stuff's been around for 3200 years and it still looks like top quality. Must have been made for a pretty water pitcher for Tut's feasts. Might have held wine too . . . Now that you ask about it, tomorrow I'll break off a piece and get it tested at the shop for its chemical composition. Might just have a batch of clay made up from the formula and send you a piece."

Dad could scarcely control his voice: "Make it in the shape of a bushing! That's a rush order, Cermak! Goodnight, you angel." The miracle had occurred: that "Tut" bushing would not explode. As Dad and I stood in the lightning lab a fortnight later he ordered the test men to fire up every available condenser that their transformers could handle. The resulting arc shook the building (and us) but didn't phase King Tut's bushing!

Within the hour President Hoover had his answer: his mighty gamble on the Colorado would pay off. The world's largest power plant could now safely send its megavolts across the forbidding Mojave desert despite its high voltage storms. The face of the earth would soon be straddled by high power lines protected by Cermak's pottery-find. God had come through. Just why He had disclosed to some forgotten potter in Tut-ankh-amen's court the precise formula needed for insulators 32 centuries later . . . just why He chose a certain marriage feast 13 centuries later for St. John to record for an engineer 19 centuries afterwards to re-read . . . just why He made the

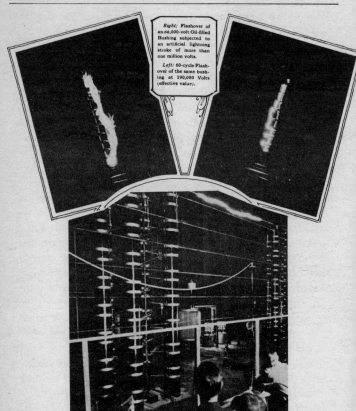

Right: Flashover of an 86,000-volt Oil-filled Bushing subjected to an artificial lightning stroke of more than one million volts.

Left: 60-cycle Flashover of the same bushing at 290,000 Volts (effective value).

MANY PTM'S saw the G-E exhibit at both fairs in '39, and both PTM'S and Testmen will work in them again this year. The above scene shows a typical crowd in Steinmetz Hall at the New York Fair watching the spectacular 10,000,000-volt bolt of artificial lightning leaping thirty feet through the air. Pittsfield Testmen ran this part of the G-E exhibit.

Sahara the setting for a drama to be completed in the Mojave . . . He alone knew then. We all know now. God's twentieth century needed His power on earth (to carry His Good News to the uttermost parts—via TV satellites unknown in the '20's).

Dad explained that God's delay in revealing an answer was for the same reason that He had waited to die on the cross when He did. *Faith*, first, then *Hope*, and *Love*. God's timing is necessarily always perfect. *Before* He died, He honored the *Faith* of His people who looked forward to His supreme sacrifice for them. *After* He died and arose, He honored the *Hope* of His people who are preparing for His return. And through *all* time He lavishes His *Love* which is the greatest gift since it abides after Faith and Hope are no longer needed.

To Dad, being a Bible-believing engineer, God's programs and promises were both logical and infallible. In fact, he claimed that without God there would be no science. His Lord invented it!

Part II

THE
MID-WEST
YEARS

MIRACLE 18

For Christ and His Kingdom

"When wisdom entereth into thine heart, and knowledge is pleasant unto thy soul, discretion shall pre-
serve thee, understanding shall keep thee; to deliver
thee from the way of evil, from the man that speak-
eth perverse things." Proverbs 2:10-12

This time had come with abrupt suddenness. Mother
was packing her little steamer trunk with my freshly laun-
dered clothes and bedding. Under them she hid a tear-
stained letter to her first son about to leave home to enter a
new life at Wheaton College out west. For her it must have
been a moment of quiet torture as she accepted the fact
that years of love and care had brought me to the age of
departure when I must fly on my own. Yet she would
always be with me in her daily moments of interceding
prayer.

When Dad had told me that he would send me to college to become trained for a medical career, I was both
excited and stunned. Two years ago The Great Crash of
'29 had wiped him out financially. Like most executives of
that day he had been lured into putting his hard-saved
dollars into stocks and investment "securities" for
"family protection." The night he came home and
quietly announced that we owned nothing but each

other's love, it had left us speechless. We held hands around the table and he talked to Heaven: "Our Father Who owns the heavens and the earth, We are like the lilies and the sparrows: we rely on You for our daily food, for our strength to grow. We don't know what to do or how to plan. I put my family into Thy care again tonight. Give them Thy heavenly riches prepared through Thine eternal love for us all. Amen."

Where he would get the tuition, Dad did not know; but he trusted the Lord for my education. Rev. Leach, now in New Jersey, had urged me three years ago after he baptized me at Hackensack to consider Wheaton College for my pre-med work. It offered uncompromising Christian principles and unquestioned high academic standards, he said. And now God had gotten me accepted, and mother had my trunk packed. Dad handed me a check for $125.00 to cover tuition and first month's costs, loaded the family in the '24 Chalmers, and said brave goodbyes at the Union station. My life as a growing boy was over: I was heading west-ward into the jaws of a depression with the confidence of ignorant youth. Only God knew the surprises ahead!

The small mid-west campus was blessed with vibrations: one kind came from the "Roaring Elgin" trains hurtling every hour to and fro on tracks a block from the famous Tower where campus engagements were announced by tolling the big bell; another came from the excited reunions of 500 campus friends colliding en route to dorms or boarding houses; and a more subtle kind of "vibes" permeated the very halls and classrooms where every professor started his lectures with a prayerful petition for an intellectual experience. I heard a rumor on my first day that twenty of the new freshmen were unsaved and that the Chapel would be left open till 10 P.M. for a group prayer meeting in their behalf! Campus life had started already: it would be a vibrating experience for sure!

My $125.00 had been promptly put in the local bank on arrival, awaiting the next Tuesday deadline for tuition payments. Not one of us was prepared for the Monday morning headlines: ROOSEVELT CLOSES BANKS! The campus was stunned. Students clustered in bewilderment seeking each other's comfort in the common disaster. The President had chosen the worst moment of the year to cripple college matriculations here and across the land. Even the College's bank accounts were frozen. There was no money available for us to return home if the College were closed!

We needed a miracle . . . and God gave it. Unknown to us the faculty and President Buswell were already praying in an emergency session in his conference room below the Tower. The college was broke. The faculty were all broke. The students were broke. What was God's advice this morning? God's answer rang clearly in that hushed room: "My promises are from everlasting to everlasting! I will never fail you. Trust Me to reopen the Banks in My own time. Run Wheaton on faith—this is your chance to witness for Me!"

I am sure that the faculty grew a foot taller in the next 30 minutes. President Buswell must have turned to Comptroller Dyrness and given an unbelievable order: "God says we stay open! Post notices that we will accept IOU's tomorrow for tuition and other dues. Notify the faculty that anyone who agrees to stay on will receive vouchers from the College. Put all the students to work on campus projects at 11 cents an hour, payable toward tuition when the banks reopen. Keep the Chapel open till midnight all month. We have let God take over this campus!"

And so it was that no one went home; no professor left his podium; nor did any campus job go begging! Never were things more spick and span—whether lawns, woodwork, windows, or bookracks. At 11 cents an hour most students could make 33 cents a day in their spare time, and that would eventually buy a textbook. I was assigned the window-washing duty at the girls' dorm—the most desirable job on campus according to my jealous classmates! Even so, I found it disappointing since none of the rooms contained the young lady whose smile had been ruining my sleep since I first spotted her singing in the Girls Chorus. Someday I would meet her in person if God wanted it that way. It was obvious that life at this college would be very different from High School; so why not pray for a miracle before the Thanksgiving exams?

Probably I shouldn't have asked God to let me be accepted into college life despite my timidity on a strange campus. When He immediately answered me, my whole program was upset. He must have known that 15 semester hours of credit-subjects was strictly the maximum load permitted without exceptional suffrage from the Dean. When I fearfully asked him for 21 hours, he looked up from his desk and said, "You sound like you mean it; sure, give it a try." I nearly tripped leaving his office: I had expected to arbitrate for 16 or 17. "God," I whispered, "don't overdo it." But He did.

At lunchtime I was lost in thought about the strange behavior of the strict Dean, when a tap on the shoulder alerted me to the smiling Junior Classman who had sat next to me in Chapel. "Aren't you Freshman Eby?" he said in a tenor voice. "I'm Charles Finney, the organist and vice-president of the Glee Club. Give me a low 'A'!" My disbelief was apparent. He laughed. "You see, I have perfect pitch and I can't believe that I heard you hit that note in chapel this morning. No one on campus for 3 years has sung that low. I need you for the College Quartet."

WHEATON COLLEGE MEN'S GLEE CLUB
-1933-

Richard—bottom row, left.
Robert—2nd row, 3rd from left.

Try as I could he would not relent. "I've never sung a note in my life aside from hymns in church and some silly songs at boys' camp," I pleaded. "I have no time or ability for Glee Club." (You guessed it: I ended up on the Quartet, with weekly rehearsals and weekend performances around the midwest. God was pouring it on.)

There was more on His docket, I found out. I had hardly gotten immersed in Chemistry 112, Chapter 2, when 5 Freshmen pounded on the stickered door. "Hey, Dick, can we come in?" "Sure, if you won't stay too long." "We hear you play a Horn and can sing," said Hall Dautel, the spokesman for some crafty scheme! "These are Les, and Pete, and Calvin, and Orien. We want you to join us as a new Gospel Team called the Melodious Messengers. We're preministerial students and play different instruments and sing a bit. I'm the organist at Rader's Tabernacle and will compose the music and set up the programs. We already voted you in!"

"Hey, fellows, it's nice to meet you but it's too late tonight for kidding. I'm pre-med. You should see my schedule, and I'm working 3 hours a day for my meals besides. There's a dozen music majors in class who will jump at the offer!"

"O.K., Dick, if you say so; but let's pray." That did it. God not only demanded that we form the group, but that I be the business manager to line up 108 concerts for the coming summer vacation. By midnight we were rehearsing our first song—and it wasn't too good.

MIRACLE 19

Melodious Messages

"Make a joyful noise unto the Lord all the earth; make a loud noise and rejoice and sing praise. Sing unto the Lord with the harp: with the harp and the voice of the psalm. With trumpets and the cornet make a joyful noise before the Lord, the King." Psalm 98:4-6

How could we college freshmen have known that the depression would last into the sophomore year? It did, and God was getting six of us ready. It was hard but fun. I doubt now that we were really aware of the extra energy He was pumping into our bodies. (Does anyone at the time?)

He enabled all six of us to survive three hours of rehearsals every night: either band, orchestra, Glee Club, or Melodious Messengers; after which we crammed in 3 to 4 hours of hard studies. Then on weekends we traveled somewhere, usually through snow or rain, to present "concerts" at churches or on the air. Of course there were hundreds of fellow students experiencing similar "witness energy" from God Who was prepared to honor their variety of endeavors to get them through the expensive college years.

One Saturday before Thanksgiving the rumor spread

6 Me-Me's = 5 "ministers" + 1 "doctor" + 3 horns + 1 God + 1 Saviour + 1 Comforter.

that some freshman girls were planning a street-corner program by the railroad tracks in downtown Wheaton. Naturally, we "Me-Me's" (Jargon for Messengers) figured we should check it out! The rumor was true: *several* lovely girls in fact! And there was *that girl* with the soprano voice, praising Jesus in song. I was scared stiff to ask her to walk back to campus with me, but Hall wasn't. After our quartet had volunteered a number, he asked her to walk with *all of us* and discuss being our vocal coach till the Spring break.

En route back, two miracles happened: Maybelle accepted our invitation to help us sound like a quartet should; and she even talked and laughed with me, the scrawniest of the group! God had something planned. Only *He* knew that she and I would ring the Tower Bell two years from then. In the meantime the quartet had a teacher, and our concerts had a "guest soloist." The

MAYBELLE ORTH
"That girl": vocal coach and guest soloist for the Melodious Messengers; who sang her way into Dick's heart!

Depression seemed to be fading away but it wasn't! We found that out when the Me-Me's pooled their spare cash to buy a car for the projected summer tour of concerts from Chicago to the east coast. We came up with $9.00 total.

How would God handle this problem? we asked Him. (It was already solved but we did not know it.) A Chicago businessman, just gone broke, had left his 7 passenger Lincoln at the junk yard in Western Springs on Saturday. Sunday night we had prayed at Wheaton; Monday morning Hall's Aunt "by chance" was driving through Western Springs and saw the car at the junk yard. That "reminded" her that she had promised Hall a car if he ever went to college! She stopped, dickered, bought it for

$25.00, and phoned her nephew to come get it! We were stunned at the news: after all, we were still youngsters at the business of watching God at work! With part of our $9.00, we then bought gas and paid a sign painter $5.00 to cover the big car with scripture verses. With the $2.00 left over, I bought stamps and paper for writing to churches a fervent prayer that they would invite us to present "The Life of Christ in Music" in return for a freewill offering. I gave no choice of dates: take it or leave it—God said it— we would be enroute and couldn't back up!

Miracles started to happen! My letters were answered saying the strangest things: mostly, "Date you requested is the only one open. See you next summer," or, "Please plan on staying for a week's meetings"; or, "We have also booked you for the local radio station; it is looking for summer talent". . . . By Memorial Day we had 108 engagements scheduled, although no one east of Chicago had ever heard of us! We didn't even have money yet to print programs and posters, and God had us booked full. He was preparing unknown audiences to share enough of their pennies and quarters to assure the Me-Me's of next year's tuition. But He was keeping that part a secret.

What we did already know was that six greener-than-grass freshman, from six widespread cities, with no prospects for summer jobs to earn Fall tuition, were singing and playing their heads off! We knew, too, that the Dean had refused to endorse our gospel team because "the College can not sanction an unknown freshman group, if you insist on going ahead with your scheme, you may only mention the College when asked where you met." However, Pres. Buswell accepted our invitation to be the Honorary Advisor.

The school year ended Friday morning with a Chapel

service. The president and dean prayed for everyone's welfare during the coming months and especially for the *upperclassmen* who would be serving as pulpit-fill-ins across the land. Six Me-Me's knew that someone must be praying for these *lowly* freshmen who were already dressed and packed to leave on their 8000-mile tour in the unknown depression land! Indeed, Maybelle and "her boarding-house gang" had God's attention: yes, He would take care of the fool-hardy King's kids. In fact, He would show them a thing or two about His ability to run a program like they had in mind! Hadn't He done pretty well so far? He had given them a tank of gas besides the car. It was time to be about His work. "Girls," He said to them, "Make them a sack lunch for the first day. After that I will feed them." (And of course, you know He did.)

MIRACLE 20

Sea of Faces

"But the Lord said unto me, Say not, I am a child: for thou shalt go to all that I shall send thee; and whatsoever that I command thee, thou shalt speak. Be not afraid of their faces; for I am with thee to deliver thee, Saith the Lord." Jeremiah 1:7,8

Fool-hardy is a useful word. No other could have so aptly described the Me-Me's as they drove off campus in the '27 Lincoln from the junk yard. The "Ark" literally ran on faith, with smooth tires and rusty plugs! But it ran. Only God's mechanical genius could explain how or why. By Sunday morning they had arrived at Church No. 1 somewhere in rural Ohio; one room with a belfry, in the middle of a corn field well off the main road! And no one was around.

God was starting us off with a real Sunday school lesson. He wanted His sextet to learn *Trust* and *Patience* the first day! I was His main target, the weakest link in the group. Being a "pre-med" had already set me somewhat apart from the others who were born-again ministerial students: Their *Call* had been clear, and their confidence was unwavering. I was sure I had faith, but I was also proud to have managed the group so well and to have lined up an amazing schedule of appearances for them.

Now we sat in an empty churchyard at 10 A.M.—apparently I had goofed on our very first day. Inwardly I quoted: "Pride cometh before a fall," and this was it.

Hall took over. "Fellows, something seems wrong in our scheduling. Let's pray, then we can take off for our evening engagement." It was so logical. We knelt against the dusty Lincoln, and thanked Jesus for getting us this far safely. He certainly had done *that* for some purpose! We had almost finished the prayer circle when a klaxon blared in our ears and someone yelled, "Hi, Fellows—glad you made it early! We had to postpone our service an hour this morning so our congregation could join the one over at Cold Springs for a brief memorial service. Their pastor died Friday, and I couldn't get word to you about the change in schedule."

God had made His point, and I felt especially small. Now I whispered another promise inside: "The Lord is Dick's Shepherd . . . He'll do the leading!" All of us turned to look down the road at the approaching "dust storm." Out of it was emerging half the cars in the county! God had collected People from miles around to attend the memorial service (probably out of respect); then for lack of anything better, He was steering them cross-country to this little church to hear a "special program from a mid-west college." People lined the aisles, sat on the window ledges, and drove their cars under the windows outside so they could sit on the fenders and listen. According to the pastor, there had never been a summer crowd like this in Green County.

And this was just the beginning! Not a week would pass without evidence of God's pre-arrangement. Just for spice, He did an extra little miracle the next day as we were hurrying along a rural brick road toward Columbus. We were half dozing when I noticed an auto wheel roll past us into the lane ahead, vault over the curb and the barbed wire fence, into the pasture and against an elm tree. Casually, I suggested to Les that he stop so I could run back and get the wheel for an extra spare since no other car had stopped for it. When I returned with the heavy wheel I noticed that our rear right was missing. Sure enough, it was our wheel. And the car was sitting perfectly level with three fellows asleep in the back! Despite the tonnage, the speed and the stopping, we were unharmed. By borrowing a lugnut from each of the other wheels, we were soon headed for the next town, and God had taught us lesson No. 2. That night we added a new testimony to our program, and God added a few more souls to His Kingdom.

MIRACLE 21

Under His Wings

"Thus saith the Lord God, Behold, I will lift up mine hand to the Gentiles, and set my standard to the people: and they shall bring thy sons in their arms, and thy daughters shall be carried upon their shoulders." Isaiah 49:22

God taught us as much between services as during them. Those ten weeks would never be duplicated; to do so would have taxed the patience of even the heavenly Father! Each event was a lesson. Some were close calls.

I well remember the day in mid-Pennsylvania when we were getting exhausted from heat and fatigue. Les was driving; the rest of us nodding or snoring. We were speeding along the upper lane of a long strip of curving highway elevated high above a mile of swampland when I suddenly sensed a change of rhythm in the tires. My eyes snapped open to see Les asleep at the wheel, and the car aimed straight ahead at a wooden guard rail some forty feet above the black swamp below. One more second and we would have disappeared from sight under the mud. At the same time I grabbed the wheel I shouted at Les to wake up: the car rode on two wheels then settled back as it found the concrete again. Les guiltily smiled and explained: "Why worry? God can steer this thing . . . Didn't He?"

Three days later we were short-cutting through back roads heading for Elmira when I sharply chided Les for cutting corners around upgrades on narrow mountain roads. He countered that he knew what he was doing, and besides God would take care of us! Just about then we shot up a grade and around the curve at the top, in the wrong lane. I sat petrified for fear of an oncoming car. Out of the corner of my eye I noted the blur of a large carton setting in the center of the righthand lane where we belonged. I jerked around to look back at whatever we had missed: and there was a child in the box waving at our disappearing car! It was minutes before I could look Les in the eye. Then with a wry grin he "enlightened" me: "Dick, you worry for nothing. Suppose if I had taken your advice and always stayed in the right lane?" I let it lie.

There was humor now and then. In Altoona we needed gas and saw a pump on the two-lane street at the curb in front of the grocery store. Down the center ran a single streetcar track. Les backed the Lincoln against the curb and started to fill the glass container atop the pump. "Hey, Les," I warned from the front seat, "our fender is over the track." "It's O.K.," came back the voice. "Not a trolley in sight." He had the tank half full when a real-to-goodness Toonerville trolley rounded the corner a block away. I can see that conductor's face now: resolute, firm, unflinching! This was his track, occupied or not. I could see the black iron knocker hit the hat-shaped gong over his head: klang, klang, klang—in perfect cadence—as the trolley pursued its deliberate crawl toward us. Like a slow nightmare it lifted the fender away from the underlying tire, pointed it "upstream," and without missing a beat on the brass gong continued its appointed journey down the street. Without a word, Les walked around the car, bent the fender back over the tire, got in and drove us off. A block away we broke into unrestrained laughter. It was like a rehearsal for an Our Gang comedy.

God had another lesson for us in Vermont. We pulled into Concord after a dusty hot day in July and found the church and parsonage both locked. None of our posters was in sight anywhere to indicate our service that night. The corner grocer suggested we try to find "old Miss Grayson at the end of the third side road past the elm beyond the creek north of town." She had taught Sunday School "for nigh 60 year." Sure enough, she was our fore-runner! As she gave us the church key, she explained that the pastor "was a modernist" and wanted nothing to do with "that Wheaton bunch," so he had left town for the week and had hidden our posters somewhere. "But I've been prayin' for ye boys to have a crowd. Ye will find some soap and water where the pipe runs into the bap-tistry. Ye look a bit dirty to me." And that we did!

Hall announced through the lather on his chin that we would rehearse some new arrangements since there would be no service. We ate the sack lunch that Miss Grayson had handed us, and the sixth man pumped the organ bellows while Hall played and the quartet fought its way through "A Mighty Fortress . . ." The reverberation in the high-vaulted church echoed our mistakes, and almost drowned out a timid knock on the front door. In the heat we were wearing only underclothes and made a dive for the dressing room behind the organ. I emerged with pants on and peered through the large keyhole in the carved maple door. There stood a crowd of kids! I swung the door half open and was greeted with a question from a casual gentleman with an emblem on his shirt.

"Is this where the musical group is performing tonight?" He obviously thought I was the janitor. "I'm Special Events Director from the Oswego Boys Camp. Our scheduled entertainment for tonight cancelled out, so I brought the boys down here. Someone had heard there was to be a concert so I took a chance. We have five bus-loads if you can seat them."

Yes, we could seat them! Through the drapes afront the unused baptistry, we watched the pews fill to over-flowing while we quickly donned our singing clothes and broke out our brass instruments. Wes, our preacher, quickly opened to Matthew 18 and reviewed his sermon material about Jesus' special love for children since they have priority in Heaven. Hall whispered the organ numbers that could be played on the old Estey, we checked our ties, and paraded onto the podium amid screams of delight from 200 throats.

God brought, so we taught. The story of Jesus as told in music held them spellbound. Wes read to them how Jesus promised eternal life in heaven to children of all ages with faith in Him. He explained how simple it was for a camper to see proof of God's handiwork everywhere, in the sky and the fields and the water. Then he suggested that any boys who wanted to know Jesus as a personal Friend should come forward so we could talk and pray about their desire to be His friends too. The angels smiled that night: boys came hurrying down the aisles, and little souls were entered into the Book of life.

Miss Grayson was elated. "Ye should know I've been praying alone for four months for ye boys to come and speak the Goss-pell! God said He'd fill the church. Sometimes I wondered, but ye came. Ye must have learned young about being good sheep and just following Him without silly bleating like some folks do. I know ye didn't get any offering for gasoline tonight, but I prayed for that too. God says ye will get a good offering in New York. Are ye headed down there?"

Yes, we were; and yes, He did supply our needs. In fact, I must tell you about those New York folks.

MIRACLE 22

Silence in the Plate

"I have coveted no man's silver or gold or apparel. Yea, ye yourselves know that these hands have ministered unto my necessities, and to them that were with me. I have showed you all things, how that so laboring you ought to support the weak, and to remember the words of the Lord Jesus, how He said, It is more blessed to give than to receive." Acts 20:33, 34, 35

New York City by nature is bewildering to an outsider. During the Depression days it was also frightening. We had booked a Sunday evening concert in the heart of "downtown" despite the warning of the skeptical pastor that he could not guarantee a crowd. Everything was against a good turnout: vacationtime, summer heat, empty pocketbooks, and above all no "big names." On Park Avenue a sextet from a little western school made no headlines, he warned. However, he would welcome us and introduce us to any of his Baptists who showed up. We could "fellowship" in his study if worse came to worse.

Hot, tired, and hungry, we arrived about 5:30 P.M. The church occupied the street level of a huge towering building, rather foreboding compared with our previous bookings. The pastor graciously ushered us into a side-room complex where we could wash and change, then we would eat. Soon he knocked and led us downstairs. It looked like a miracle: a great banquet room filled with applauding "pot-luckers"! Women in aprons were scurrying around with trays of food unlike any we had seen on our depression menus. People crowded around to welcome the "westerners" and apologize for the other thousand who could not be there. Ladies explained that the Depression "problem" only permitted this pot-luck instead of a real dinner! Our grace over heaping platters was an inadequate "Thankyou, God, for being so good."

When we "retired upstairs" to the main auditorium, we found it filled with more people than we usually faced in a whole week. The pastor was bewildered too: he figured that the crowd could not afford vacations this year so they stayed home and came to "benefits." He didn't know about Miss Grayson in Vermont, nor about her prayers for "ye boys."

When collection-time came, the pastor's eloquence rose to new heights! He and God had a captive audience, and he intended to offset his original doom and gloom prediction. "Brothers and Sisters, these boys have come a long ways and they need all God's money that is in your pockets. Now one thing we do not tolerate in Park Avenue Baptist is noise during the offering! Tonight will be a silent offering. Let no coin jingle during Hall Dautel's organ interlude. God's land is green: so must be your giving! Let your praise equal His providence. God, we thank you for these gifts!"

There was very little noise during Dautel's interpretation of "Master, The Tempest Is Raging." For once he didn't break an ivory on the keyboard: the organ was up to his thunder! We gasped as we counted "Miss Grayson's promise" after the service. $528.25. More than the whole collection to date. God was really real: we could pay off the printer, buy a whole tank of gas at a time, and eat breakfast regularly. There was enough to buy a roll of film for Orien's camera, and retread the two bald tires. And God was withholding a secret at the same time. Enough was enough, now.

Labor day found us back on campus. God had fed us, steered our car, kept us from being shot by cops in Philadelphia who mistook us for fleeing hoodlums, given us souls, and brought us back! One thing mystified us: after dividing the unspent collection moneys, we had only enough for books and nothing for tuition. Since God had provided every other need, why would He stop short at tuition? We huddled in a final prayer to ask His solution. Should we disband tomorrow and thumb our way back home? Was that His will for us Me-Me's? Something told us to wait till tomorrow for the answer. We each needed the $150.00 fee. Tomorrow was the deadline, and it must be in cash—no IOU's this year!

Hall received the answer first: during breakfast the Dean noticed him across the room and dropped over to mention that a letter from New York was being held for him in his office—for the past three weeks, in fact. "Probably not important, but drop up for it after you finish that blueberry muffin." Hall really thought it was a ruse to get him in private where the Dean could offer "official regrets" for his being unable to re-register for the Fall class. It was noon before he got courage to face the music. The envelope was scrawled with no return address. He half-heartedly tore it open, and a yellow check dropped on the floor. He picked it up in amazement as he read the amount: $900.00! Quickly he pulled out a yellowing piece of note paper with a shakily scrawled message: "Dear Melodius Messengers: I am an old lady in New York who heard your music at the Baptist Church. I am nearly blind now so I can not use this money for my usual round the world trip this year. Something told me today that you boys need a bit more help than we gave you here. Mr. Dautel, would you please divide this little gift so you can each have $150.00 toward your education? You must'nt know my name now. Soon I will be in heaven. When we all meet there we won't need anything except our voices to sing praises. I hope I have helped you nice young men."

God had written His final sanction to our summer's experiment in faith! We would stay in college. Each Me-Me would graduate to serve as called: five ministers and a physician. Each would become useful locally and nationally. All would find helpmates right on campus. God was indeed all He claimed—on campus and off. In the years to come He would do wonders for all of them.

The Return of the "Messengers"

Toward evening on Monday, September 13th, the weather-beaten tower of Wheaton College outlined by an overcast sky, seemed to welcome silently and majestically the Melodious Messengers at the conclusion of their first Eastern tour. Turning down a side street before going on to the campus,

The Melodious Messengers, one of the student groups that spent the summer in Christian service. These men were all members of last year's freshman class. Front Row, left to right, Hall Dautel, Orien G. Johnson. Back Row, left to right, Calvin Busch, Lawrence Eyres, J. Lester Harnish, Richard E. Eby.

"The Ark," as the car was familiarly known to the boys, was brought to a standstill and, as Noah made an offering unto God, they stopped to make a praise-offering to their heavenly Father.

Where could they begin? They praised the Lord for "The Ark" He had given them; for health and strength to carry on; for the fact that He was pleased to use their small abilities and talents; for the miraculous protection and guidance which kept them from accidents over the seventy-four hundred miles; for the friends who were given to them; for the opportunity to give their message of "The Life of Christ—in Music" in ninety-eight churches; for allowing them to broadcast the message from twelve different radio stations and to hold meetings in boys' and girls' camps all over the East; for the large crowds and for the small crowds, always remembering that Jesus preached to just one woman in Samaria and many believed.

They praised God for the services that were held on the board-walks at Atlantic City and Wildwood, N.J., where those who came looking for "something for nothing" found Him who gives the water of life freely to "whosoever will."

They praised Him for the wonderful meeting that was conducted in a church in Claremont, N. H., where men and women, some of whom had never heard the Gospel, accepted Christ as their personal Saviour.

Part III

THE
CALIFORNIA
YEARS

MIRACLE 23

Diplomate and Roommate

For the Lord giveth wisdom; out of His mouth cometh knowledge and understanding. He layeth up
sound wisdom for the righteous; He is a buckler to
them that walk uprightly." Proverbs 2:6, 7

I had asked God to give me wisdom in choosing a
medical school which would fit *my* needs, not just the
ideas of my several friends who naturally suggested only
the Big Names in the healing business. I had really
expected to be called as a missionary—with India especially on my mind, perhaps because of the dedicated
people who had visited our home from Bombay, Cal-
cutta, and other towns in that sorry land.

Always I felt an inward "NO" to that idea; instead,
"Seek Medicine!" So I interviewed doctors from different Colleges. Strangely, only the D.O.'s gave me the
time of day; they were enthusiastic about their holistic,
structure-function concepts of medicine. They were often
ridiculed but still were getting results, they said, after
other approaches had failed! The course was four long
years, actually five crammed into four, they explained. I
was also impressed to find that each one believed that God
had a large part to play in all processes of healing. In fact,
they pointed out, the Osteopathic profession had been

founded by a medical missionary's son, himself one until he opened his college in Missouri. My investigations led me to write to the Los Angeles College. Imagine my surprise to get an answer from the President: he reminded me (as though I would remember) that he had helped operate me on the kitchen table years ago! If my grades were O.K., he wanted me there for sure. Although I could have chosen large eastern Universities, I felt led to Los Angeles. Horace Greeley had said "Go West, young man, go West"; I did, and it proved good for me.

Those were four long, hard years of study into wee morning hours. My 71 classmates were fine men and women, albeit of assorted varieties. We were all poor, but dedicated to become the best possible doctors like many of our faculty most of whom donated their time and talents. (At our 40th reunion in 1977 we could count and recount hundreds of man-years of devoted patient care provided by our depression class. However, many were quitting practice because they refused to charge the high fees required to pay for the "malpractice" insurance as protection from money-hungry ingrates. Society was the loser.)

God wouldn't let me become a book-worm recluse, even with so much study to complete every day. I was asked to direct a youth choir in Whittier, and to sing in a church quartet besides. When someone heard that I was a horn player they enlisted me at the Church of the Open Door. God said "Good!" That way I would hear His Word spoken at least once a week.

Campus activities were demanded of me despite other chores: (a small voice kept reminding me that a well-rounded doctor could serve better than a tunnel-vision genius)! So I served my school and class as an officer, honor society president, library chairman, newsbulletin and Annual editor, plus assorted assignments from administration heads. Years later, sitting as College president in Missouri, I thanked my God for those bone-wearying days of preparation to understand better how a student thinks and reacts to pressures.

Finally graduation was three months away, and I had finished my work already in order to visit my parents in New England, and especially to see my lady-love who had warded off a parade of suitors during the long four years of separation. (In 1937 marriage was only for those who could afford a wife: and I was broke.) We often laugh now when I state that I started practice with a patient woman and ended it with women patients.

Two weeks before graduation my parents beame ill with different problems. Desperately I wrote President Phinney to suspend the hard-and-fast rule that "no diploma can be granted unless the candidate is in attendance at graduation exercises." I learned later that an emergency conference was called, and the rule was suspended: I became the only graduate in its 33 years to be granted a college diploma in absentia! I am sure that my God whispered into ears that day.

My next joy was the notice a week later that I had been chosen No. 1 on the list of successful applicants for a County Hospital internship, the biggest prize in the city; Dr. O'Meara hoped I could make it, though it meant returning from New England. I prayed that my folks would get well. They did, and I made it!

Naturally, I stopped over at Chicago to say another goodbye to Maybelle. I told her that I was releasing her from this long engagement; it just wasn't fair to ask her to wait another two long years while I was earning

$10/month at the "County." She refused to listen: somehow God would work it out, she promised, so that she could join me in California. She would pray about it. Tearfully, we waved goodbye at the Bus Station not knowing what lay ahead.

The new interns were sternly told that the shifts were "36 on and 12 off" (hours, that is). And no need to ask for favors! When anyone got sick, the others had to double up on the coverage. All beds were filled every day. "Thirty minutes off for meals if you can stand the food." Usually we couldn't.

In mid-November the phone at the charting desk rang and I casually put it to my ear while I continued writing an "H & P" on a new patient's chart. "I'm in Omaha; see you in 48 hours, my love!" She giggled at having pulled a "fasty." 'You're what?" I blurted. "Just thought I'd let you know: I'm marrying you on your next day off. Can't wait forever, you know; you can stand a good cook, can't you?" The operator cut in: "Sorry, emergency call coming in. Hang up."

I was on duty when her train pulled into L.A. My out-of-a-job uncle drove her from the station to the Hospital, and I had both a joy and a problem on my hands! I pled my case before the Medical Director: "Can't you bend a rule even once?" I demanded. "My fiancee just arrived, unexpected! I have a one-room apartment and neighbors with gossipy tongues. It won't do your reputation any good if a beautiful single girl moves in with a bachelor intern. At least give me Saturday afternoon off to get married! I'll only do it once."

He grimaced. "They'll get me for this, but I see your logic! I'll give you two hours off. Be back by six—or else. After all, the 'County' isn't in the marriage business."

That was that—better than nothing. I dialed my Wheaton classmate, now a pastor at a South Western Avenue Church, and asked his price for tying a knot. "Scot-free for you, Dick," he laughed. "After all, I could have had her if you hadn't been around!" "Then I can afford you if you don't accept tips," I replied. "See you 4:30 Saturday sharp."

A year and a half later we looked back and laughed. It was obvious by then that God did supply needs. From somewhere we had been given just enough to be housed and fed every week with two nickels left over for carfare to go window shopping: it made daydreaming about the future seem less imaginary. Someday we might even have a spare $2 to spend for fun: we did! We blew it on a Second Anniversary dinner at the San Carlos Hotel in Monterey: their "Extra-special Chateaubriande-for-Two—5 course meal—$2.00 no tax."

Of course, our immediate problems were real: where to find a place to practice and how to know when we had found it! God knew that an easy answer never builds faith, so He let us work on it together.

MIRACLE 24

Eleventh Hour Answers

"Wherefore take no thought, saying, What shall we eat? or What shall we drink, or wherewithal shall we be clothed? . . . For your Heavenly Father knoweth that you have need of all these things." Jesus speaks in Matthew 6:31, 32

God had plans for us but we did not listen soon enough. Like most young doctors finishing their training programs we were anxiously searching for a stable location where we could survive economically while "practicing" our skills. After a year of internship at $10/month, followed by a residency at $25/month, we were ready to grasp at straws.

The 1939 economy in California was at its lowest. Every established doctor discouraged us from moving into his territory since he could barely make a living already. Try as I could, not one welcome reply could I evoke from months of correspondence up and down the State. However, from Detroit there was a welcome bid to join the staff of the Detroit Osteopathic Hospital where obstetrics was becoming a renowned service.

With only a month of Residency training left at Los Angeles, we borrowed money for a rail ticket for Maybelle to travel east, with a stop for a visit at Chicago, then proceed to Detroit to find an office for me. With my little steamer trunk and her hand-me-down suitcase I bid her goodbye with a prayer for her success and safety. I would follow when I got my severance pay in a month. We wondered what lay ahead.

Two mornings later I was summoned to the Medical Director's office. Such summons usually implied a serious "goof": naturally, I was apprehensive. Dr. O'Meara, a solidly built, greying gentleman, was the perfect figure of a competent administrator who seldom called anyone to his private office until he had "the facts straight." I squared my skinny shoulders and turned the knob.

His greeting was pleasant. "Come in, Richard. Have a seat ... I was just checking your employment record with us. You haven't asked to stay on. Is there a reason? You know you are No. 1 on our rating list, and we would like you to stay!" My spirits rose.

"Thank you for your kind invitation, Chief. It has been a great experience to serve under you, but my wife and I must find some way to eat!" I laughed and squeezed my arm. "You know, she didn't get much of a bargain marrying this bag of bones; I'm not much over my birth weight after eating county food in your Taj Mahal!"

He joined my laughter. "That's what I thought. I have an offer for you. I've been looking for two years for the right man to take over my former office in Monterey. It is a delightful community ... were you ever there? No? ... well, it has potential for a pioneer like you. A little Bayside Hospital. Cannery Row. A presidio. Working people. And a few wealthy ones in Carmel over the hill. Eby, you could be making $250/month by Christmas— that's ten times what we pay here!"

He watched my cautious reaction. "And I will see

that you get hired by the Police Department for their emergency work; they pay promptly in cash—50 cents a call; that's even better than the 40 cents at the office—sometimes on the cuff. Let me loan you $5.00 for a bus ticket; go up there Saturday and look it over. I'll get Dr. Robison to cover for you. A deal?"

"I'll let you know tomorrow, Chief. Thanks a million for your confidence. My wife is halfway to Detroit right now to look for a possible spot there. This takes some thought." I was in a mental fog the rest of the day. What would Maybelle think if I suddenly changed our life's plans and asked her to return to a "site unseen"? By morning I had my answer: for $5.00 and a day off I would at least look at Monterey. What could I lose?

Dr. O'Meara was excited to learn of my decision to check out his old office. "Richard, here's your $5.00. I phoned my brother last night, and he will meet you at the Custom's House and take you home for the night. In fact, he'll rent you his home if you agree to take over the office. He has some entertainment planned already; he's excited for you to take over his practice because he just got hired on yesterday at a clinic in L.A. starting next week. Everything's working out as I had hoped!" It was obvious that the cagey old Chief had been making plans for some time!

Yes, Monterey was beautiful. No bluer bay in the world. Redwoods, pines, and "butterfly trees." Gently lapping waves along miles of sandy beaches. Picturesque sardine boats and "one-lunger" fishing boats rocking at anchor. And a Japan current that boiled a mile offshore. No wonder Steinbeck used it as a stage for his cannery novels and Okey tales!

My bones were tired from jolting 350 miles in the ancient bus (the new ones were apparently going to Europe for troop use): but Dr. Gene didn't slow down. I had to be shown everything in a hurry before a mad dash to Salinas as guests at the Policeman's Ball. There was the third floor office, and the 17-mile Drive with its ritzy mansions and shore-side golf course, and the dozens of historic buildings which had colored the lifestyle in California's first capital. And Cannery Row, world's largest sardine center (and biggest free smell of a fish smorgasbord!).

The Policeman's Ball was something else. My first time away from the Hospital for two years was a sudden exposure to life on the outside as it had developed under the cloud of Hitler's war overseas. I had never seen 200 blue uniforms on a night off, letting off steam. I was welcomed like royalty: "Look, the first new doctor in years; boy, can we use him. Can you start tomorrow? Here, have a drink." "No thanks," I volunteered; "I never drink on duty, and I am never off when I work for you fellows."

It was the first complete meal I had eaten for a year (on an income of 75 cents a day Maybelle and I had learned to enjoy 10 cent meals). I could still breathe after the dessert, but not deeply. Then the Captain tapped me on the arm and whispered, "Here comes the good stuff!" and so it (she) did. Spinning in graceful circles through a side doorway emerged an exquisitely built Mexican senorita. As she spun under the spotlight in center stage the whistles and catcalls drowned out the castinettes: she had left her clothes offstage, as well as any modesty. In the Hospital this was a common sight, but in a restaurant setting, in violent motion, when laws made public nudity a strict No-No on earth, she was greeted as a heavenly body! I wondered if this After-Dinner-Delight was a prediction of American standards 30 years from then.

Hardly had the cock crowed when Dr. Gene rushed

me off for a final round of sightseeing. He showed me the rows of modest "New Monterey" homes where the Cicilian and Mexican Cannery workers lived overlooking the old wooden buildings and wharves long since saturated with fish oil. We drove past the Presidio barracks where a century of history had been woven into California's changing succession of flags. In Seaside we saw the squalid huts of broken boards, corrugated tin, and cardboard siding where the Okeys and Arkies lived in comparative comfort to the dust bowl life from which they had escaped. And then next door we saw how the wealthy folks lived at the Hotel Del Monte with its manicured grounds, golf course, and parking lot full of limosines with their cut-glass flower vases and chromed tire covers. On the front lawn in regal procession we watched impeccably gowned ladies and gentlemen of rank walking their pointed-eared, stiff-tailed canines past a ribbon-bedecked judge. It was obvious that Monterey "had everything." I was ready to tackle it. I phoned Maybelle that a miracle had happened: a practice, an office, a house, and a beautiful waterfront for my favorite sport, fishing!

She finally got a word in edgewise: "Wonderful! I'll change my ticket to the San Francisco Zephyr and take the Monterey Flyer. I think I should stay here a couple of weeks longer till I feel a little better." I interrupted: "A little better? Did you get sick on the train?" "I guess so. My stomach is upset. Of course I am excited over seeing my family here, and the weather is so hot and muggy too. Don't worry; I can't wait to help you get the new office going. I love you."

Three weeks later we celebrated her arrival. I had discovered a little shanty-sized restaurant on the wharf with the largest prawn salads I had ever seen. I told the

Italian chef to make two especially good ones that day for "the new Doc and his Lady," and I would give him 25 cents each instead of the usual 15 cents listed on the menu! We said a quick blessing to the rhythm of the gentle waves slapping against the pilings below our chairs, and looked up to see two huge beautiful shrimp salads. I waited to see her joy over the first bite: instead, a frown.

"It looks so delicious, Dick, but would you mind if I just enjoy the view?" Suddenly I was suspicious that she had something to tell me, but that she wanted me to tease it out of her.

"Of course, the view is delightful—famous too," I countered. "But not every wife turns down her favorite food so casually! Not unless she is becoming a mother! 'Fess up. Are you trying to tell me that you plan to start calling me Daddy? Really?"

She grabbed for my neck. "Oh yes, Daddy. I thought you would never ask."

God had done it again: prepared an abode, a practice, an opportunity to grow—just when we had need of help—at the eleventh hour. We would fully realize His method of supplying needs in the years to come: He always waited till the last minute to reveal His answer: if He didn't, we could not learn FAITH!

MIRACLE 25

Life is Like a Mountain Railroad

"Notwithstanding she shall be saved in childbearing if they (she) continue in faith and charity and holiness with sobriety." I Timothy 2:15

Almost two years at Monterey had passed: busy, happy, learning years. Every day was exciting to see little Walter rapidly outgrow his crib and toddle between the stroller and the toy box, either pushing, throwing, or restacking according to the demands of the moment. Helping Da-Da smooth the sand around Ma-Ma's row of geraniums was a happy challenge too. Sitting on the window ledge became a ritual in the morning when the purse seiners glided like huge swans out of the blue bay en route to the sardine schools offshore. Walter would try to imitate the baritone blasts of their fog horns as they echoed along the peninsula, and would squeal with delight when one seemed to answer him.

God had supplied the house and furnishings several months ago when an emergency had arisen. In the midst of the turmoil of Walter's arrival, with the extra expenses, the disturbances in office appointments, the changes in hospital schedules, and extra time needed to take care of household items while Maybelle was recovering from her cesarean, I received notice that we would be evicted from the cottage which we were then renting from its owner living in South America. Due to business reverses (possibly secondary to the ballooning war in Europe) the owner was returning to Monterey in about six weeks and would want his house upon arrival. (You can imagine the bombshell reaction upon opening his letter.) We prayed, then went looking for the answer.

Our $45 Studebaker stalled every few blocks, but I jiggled the carburetor float and off we went each time. There was not a single house for rent anywhere. The rumor that a "Fort Ord" had been proposed for Monterey in case "World War II" involved the U.S.A. had brought hundreds of hopeful workers and families flocking from the east and south. I had saved my 40 cent office fees until we had about $30 left after hospital and living expenses were paid. Certainly we could not afford more than a cheap rental at the most.

Discouraged after several days of looking, we had a sudden "inspiration" Saturday afternoon to pull to the curb as we drove past a new house under construction in Pacific Grove. The carpenter was standing on the sidewalk admiring his roofing job; he might know of a house for rent if the new owners of this one were vacating an old one. We would ask.

He acted like he expected us and had known us for some time! "Hello folks! And what a cute baby you have there! I figured a young couple like you would want this house." He grinned as though his sale were in the bag.

"We surely do need one," I replied, "if you know of a cheap one for rent. I figured you might direct us to a house being vacated by someone moving into a new one. Any chances?"

Before he spoke he was already shaking his head.

"Not a one. No one has an extra dime to put on a new house so they are all renting old ones." He paused and looked us over again. "You look honest. Maybe *you* can help *me* . . . I'm in trouble too. I borrowed money last week for a load of lumber for my next house, thinking I had this one sold; the deal fell through. Today I've just decided to sell this house to the next party with enough money to pay the ecrow fees, with nothing down. Then I can use the bank money to meet the lumber bill next week. Do you know anyone with $29.85 who needs a new house?"

Maybelle and I exchanged glances. She knew we had $30 in the bank. I was thinking, What's the use of praying if we reject the answer? I had him repeat his offer; I had heard him right the first time. "I'll be back in an hour to let you know if I can find someone to help you," I blurted. I jiggled the carburetor and made a U-turn, down the street and into the parking lot at a furniture store. Maybelle was aghast: "What are you doing, Dick?" "I want to talk to the owner here. He goes to our church. I have an idea."

"Hello, Doc," he greeted me, "nice to see the wife and kid today in the store. You must have heard that our big sale starts Monday! Pick today, pay on time. You can be my first 'sale' customer: always half price to Number 1, you know." He face was beaming as though he was Santa Claus handing gifts to little kids.

"Can you outfit a 2-bedroom house including baby furniture and washing machine for a figure that I can handle real cheap? I'm just getting started, and 'most everything's on the cuff!"

"Why, sure. Could you handle $34 a month on a loan? Give me two weeks to make delivery, after the sale's over, and I'll make your home look like a doctor's little mansion!'' He was already excited over whatever he had in mind for us. Like a dashboard doggie, my head started to nod assent. Why not a new house and new furnishings if that was God's answer—again at His eleventh hour!

That day we had taken a new plunge into faith. Now, nearly a year and a half later we were a ''settled couple'' in our own home; and every time that we had needed money to meet the bills, unexpected patients had dropped into the office or hospital to cover our needs. And Maybelle was expecting our second child: she had ordered a girl, and had no doubt that the pink layettes were the right color! She silenced dubious friends by reminding them that Jesus promised to supply answers whenever we asked and believed that we would receive! They would wait and see, they said.

In the dark she poked me awake. ''Daddy, this is the day our daughter wants out,'' she announced as I yawned. Sure enough, I could confirm her cramps, but they were intestinal rather than uterine. Besides, she had a fever. ''Do you feel nauseated, Honey?'' I asked. ''Yes, most of the night, and some diarrhea too, but it must be the baby's pressure, don't you suppose?'' No I didn't. With two weeks remaining till her due date for a repeat cesarean she had obviously contracted the epidemic enteritis that was rampant around the Bay. Many were seriously ill and in hospitals. We didn't know, lying there in the dark, that our faith was being tested once again.

That was a horrible day for her, and bad enough for me. My nurse cancelled the appointments so I could stay home to care for her and Walter. Her fever and cramping worsened, along with the diarrhea and vomiting. Nothing seemed to work right. Walter became upset at the sudden change in his daily routine without his mother's knowing attentions. By afternoon new cramps were developing—this time my fears were confirmed: the intestinal "flu" was starting her labor prematurely, and she was awfully sick, really a bad risk for surgery. I called her surgeon in Salinas, and then our stand-by baby-sitter to care for Walter, and we headed for the hospital 35 miles away.

(Thinking back now, we realize that God must permit big problems to develop in order to provide Big Answers. In our young lives, as in so many others, He must teach lessons of faith early enough for us to get "real mileage" out of them as we grow older. He is such a perfect teacher when it comes to timing and methods!)

Surgery did not go smoothly despite my prayers as I waited for news in the reception room. Her fever and dehydration and exhaustion had made the anesthetic difficult, I was soon to learn. Suddenly a nurse burst through the swinging doors and asked if I knew how to give an anesthetic. I nodded and she grabbed me and headed for the dressing room. "Quick," she blurted, "Gown and get into surgery. You're needed!" She left without any explanation. "God," I asked, "what goes?" and dashed into the ether-filled arena.

A nurse thrust an ether can into my hands and pointed to my wife's grey face. "Here, keep her asleep. The anesthetist is working with your daughter in the nursery to get her breathing. Dr. Slater is starting his closure. Here's the oxygen tube." I checked her weak pulse and shallow respirations. Too deep already—nearly fourth stage! "Jesus," I silently screamed, "don't let me crack up now. Save them both, please."

It seemed like hours before the surgeon turned to me and pulled off his gloves. "A rough one," he conceded.

"She can't have any more children—too much scar tissue. I'll go see if the baby is making it while you get her stabilized." I was already thanking my Healer for the training I had been given in Los Angeles under a fine anesthetic staff. I had somehow felt stone calm, suddenly, as I had gently nudged her failing respiratory center back to a steady function during the past hour. Now her color was normal though her pulse was fast from fever. She would soon be awakening. I wondered what lay ahead as I hurried to the nursery.

Little Carol (long ago named at Christmas time) lay weak but pink. The anesthetist was needlessly apologetic: "It took so much ether to relax your wife's muscles due to her fever that the baby went to sleep before Dr. Slater could get her out. Luckily that kept her from breathing till we could thoroughly clear her throat of mucus. She'll do fine now." I thanked him and hoped that his future cases would do better; after all, I thought, maybe he is learning too. I was suddenly tired, very tired.

God was not yet through with His lesson on Faith. As I wearily pulled into my driveway two hours later there stood my neighbor's husband. He asked about Maybelle then explained his presence: "Your baby-sitter got a call just after you left that her father in San Luis Obispo was dying from a sudden stroke. She had to take off. My wife and I have been watching the boy. We hope that's alright. We'll help out till Maybelle gets home." Thank God for that answer, I whispered. Now what's next?

The phone was ringing at 2 P.M. as I entered the office. An urgent voice blurted in my ear: "This is the Salinas Hospital. Dr. Slater says come quick; your wife is dying." The line went dead. Again, I had nowhere else to turn: "Please, Jesus, keep her alive till I can get there and say goodbye if you must take her home." This time I broke the speed laws. For some unknown (?) reason the highway was open for 35 miles; not a patrol car nor a broken down lettuce truck! I was there in 22 minutes.

Jesus had beat me there, praise His Name! The nurse grabbed me as I rushed down the hall and pulled me to a halt: "Ten minutes ago Mrs. Eby suddenly revived and started to breathe again. She seems alright now!" I pushed through the door and saw her face, pallid but somehow aglow. At my touch she smiled and murmured, "Would you believe it, Honey, I was just in Heaven!" She took another breath. "I met my father there on a train headed down the valley toward the Holy City. It was so beautiful."

She squeezed my hand and hurried on. "I could feel myself dying a while ago after the nurse fed me that stuffed bell pepper. I was too sedated to refuse it, and right away I began to fill with gas. It pushed up under my chest till everything went black and I was in Heaven. Dad looked so happy—not tired and sick like when he died. He had his conductor's uniform on, and we sang 'Life is Like A Mountain Railroad." That was his favorite."

Another squeeze, and then: "He insisted I stay with him, but I told him about the children, and how I must go back to take care of them. I kept pulling away from his hugging arms, and then he suddenly let me go, and I am back with you!" Like a contented lamb, she fell off to sleep.

The nurse later explained everything "scientifically." The accidental meal had produced immediate acute indigestion with distention. The diaphragmatic compression had produced cardiac arrest with resultant agonal relaxation of all sphincters. She had literally exploded from both ends as the nurses had franticly applied oxygen and resuscitative measures to the apparent dead body. The doctor had arrived just as she started breathing a bit, and had them call me "just in case she dies again." I thanked her for her explanation, and suggested that our Lord may have arranged the meal, the distention, the arrest, the explosion, and the visit with her late father for some eventual purpose. She smiled and shrugged: "I'm glad *something* saved her." I was too!

Years later the Lord used her story of that day to win souls and comfort hearts. Every miracle has a purpose—at some time.

Interlude

"But the Comforter, the Holy Ghost, whom the Father will send in My name, he will teach you all things and bring all things to your remembrance, whatsoever I have said unto you." Jesus in John 14:26

In retrospect it should have been impossible to survive as a new boyish-looking doctor in poverty stricken pre-war Monterey! Although England was buying up every shipload of "pilchards" for its troops, little of that money filtered back to the workers on Cannery Row. I was soon to learn that paychecks were issued on a seasonal basis—*maybe* once every 3 to 6 months. In the meantime business was done on the cuff. There was one obvious blessing to this arrangement however: we carried on a practice without mentioning money. The honest ones would bring it in later, and the others wouldn't have paid anyway!

Out of this relaxed form of economy came some unexpected laughs—frosting as it were on the cake of life (the only one cheap enough to relish). I must share a few memories from my mental scrapbook (or scrapheap?). They were all for free! Some contained little sermons along with the laughs.

INCIDENT ONE

It was my first week in private practice, and I wanted everything to go right and proper. I could sense that the community was sizing up "the young doctor" who had moved into a medical fraternity where seniority had long since produced a closed shop for newcomers. My $10/month office had two rooms: one for reception, and another for treatment.

The second day a sweet voice on the phone informed me that she had been getting "back treatments" for some time, and needed to get in immediately for another. Since my book was empty, I said I could see her by 4 P.M. She stepped through the door exactly at 4, and what a vision! Twenty-two with eyes of blue. And a photographer's dream. "Where is your nurse?" she asked, noting we were alone. "I'm still interviewing applicants this week," I answered honestly. "Well, that's fine," she volunteered. "I'll get ready for my treatment." "Yes," I said, "You'll find a gown on the table. Knock on the door when you're ready." I stepped out into the reception room, and she was already knocking. There she stood stark naked, as beautiful a pink statue as could be imagined. At her feet lay her single garment, and on her face a smile of anticipation. I could almost see Satan leering in the corner. "You forgot your gown," I suggested. "It opens down the back. Knock again when you're ready," and I closed the door. This time her face said "Well?" as she stood with the gown opened in front to expose her figure. "Your front looks well," I said by way of diagnosis, "But I need to check your back. Try once again to put it on right." With a pout she closed the door and spoke to it or through it: "I never had to wear one before; it gets in the way!" This time things were proper and I could check her back (though nothing seemed to be wrong as I felt along the well-formed spine). "If you're through," she said, "let's have our drinks. I feel so relaxed!"

"But, Miss Tucker, I don't take patients to the bar," I exclaimed. "Of course not," she replied, "we keep everything here." "Here? Where?" I blurted. She hopped off the table, dropping her gown expertly, and opened a previously locked wall cabinet which I had assumed contained the previous renter's personal effects. She obviously had unlocked it while gowning. It was a miniature bar with expensive name brands and glasses. "Which do you prefer, Honey?" she asked, fingering the various options. I shook my head in disbelief. "I'm going to make you a present," I said, lifting the gown back over her squatting figure: "You take all those bottles home but don't say where you got them. Pay me 50 cents for the examination, and we'll consider you cured."

She pulled on her dress over her head and handed me a dollar bill. My wallet fell open as I took out change, revealing to her a photo of my wife. "Oh, you already have a girl friend," she gasped: "but you're so young!" "Yes, and she wears a band ring very proudly," I commented pointedly. "Well, Doctor, I won't need to make another appointment." She wiggled her hips to test the motion. "I think you have cured my back problem."

It was several weeks before Maybelle or I could say "back-ache" without laughing. We agreed that our general practice would not be dull, not in Monterey at least!

INCIDENT TWO

The 3 P.M. appointment was to be my first case of

voluntary amnesia. A stiff-spined lady entered the office almost dragging a frightened 15 year old daughter with an obviously enlarged abdomen. "For 6 months I have been telling her to stop eating so much," she railed. "Doctor, I insist you give her reducing pills to get this weight off immediately! Can you promise to reduce her fast?" I smiled as I saw the baby's vigorous kicking through her thin skirt. "Yes, I can promise. Give me a week or two . . . By the way, could she be expecting a baby?" "Of course not!" the mother snapped back. "Preposterous. She does not even know how babies are made! She is simply fat."

I winked at the girl: "You might tell your mother why your dress is jumping." "She knows; I'm just loaded with gas. Why, I don't even know what a boy looks like, do I, Mother?" "Of course not. Preposterous!" I suddenly realized that they both believed their own deceptions so I explained that they should head for the Hospital when her "gas pains" became regular or unbearable in the next week or so. They were delighted when I gave her some pills for her "swelling." Ten days later I reduced her of a squalling 8 pound "swelling," and suddenly they remembered something that each had "forgotten." It was really a laugh after all: even the swelling smiled.

INCIDENT THREE

"Come down to the Station, Doc," the Police Captain drawled. "Got a call from the railroad flophouse. The patrolman will take you over to see what's up." It was 1 A.M., foggy and cold, but it was 50 cents so I rolled out of my comfortable hideout. We found the door ajar to the ancient shed which had been converted into sleeping quarters long ago. A single bulb midway down the long hall illuminated the opposing row of doorways. A phone dangled from the wall. We listened at each door for a sign of life, till we heard some snores. The "Cop" cautiously pushed the door open and snapped on his flashlight. We laughed at the sight.

Curled like a poorly wrapped mummy lay a ragged-dressed Methusela on a broken bedspring cot. A bedside stand made of apple boxes and an orange crate completed the furnishings, and supported an empty fifth of White Horse. It was like a movie set from Paradise Lost. "Wake up, old man. Come on now. You can't sleep like this." The patrolman kept shaking the bag of bones as the snoring changed its cadence. The eyes slowly emerged from between sticky lids, and the snores became grunts of surprise. "Unh, Unh. Hey. Whaja want?"

"Was it you who phoned for a Doc?" I asked. "Yeah, you one?" he sputtered. "I couldn't get to sleep so I called the cops. Ain't they my frands?" We laughed at the logic. "Sure thing. But you were sure sleeping fine just now. What happened?"

"Well, I'm a God-fearing man with ulcers. You know about ulcers? They hurt bad tonight so I broke my vow about drinking and took a half of a fifth to settle 'em down. Gad, how it burned. So I took the rest. Musta gawn to sleep." He gave us a toothless grin and stuck out a boney hand toward me. "You're a great Doc. Feel better already! Say, did I pay you yet?" He fumbled at the orange crate. "Now, Doc, I allays pays ma debts. Look in the top drawer and take as many bills as you need for getting me well tonight. Right there in the corner." Curiosity prompted me to look. A small wooden match-box with "Lucifer" across it was the only item there. Inside were 5 bone-hard, black (and ancient) raisins. "Is this your money, Dad?" I asked. "Yes sirree. Now you take what you need and leave me the rest," he ordered with a shake of his boney finger. "Yah know, I all-ays pays me debts."

It took a half hour to bundle him up and get him back to the warmth of the Police Station. Our routine "frisk" for identification turned up a wrinkled business card from a Cleveland, Ohio dental office: and that was not all! In his trouser seams were sewn $490 in assorted bills—a veritable fortune for anyone in 1940!

We let the phone ring quite a while in Cleveland before we got a voice back: "Who is this?" I asked. "Dr. Barry, a sleepy dentist. Who wants me at this hour?" I laughed: "The Monterey police in California want you . . ." He interrupted: "Oh, not again! You have old Dad out there? He ran away again last week, and we've been waiting to learn where he would turn up. Does this every now and then since he passed 90. Loves to ride the rails. He keeps money in his pant's seams. Cut some out and buy him a ticket back home. He'll give you no trouble. . . . By the way, Thanks a lot, Doc." The next day I too was sleepy.

INCIDENT FOUR

On foggy nights the phone rang most often. Especially about 2 A.M. Wearily, I picked it up and listened: "Doc, you've gotta come. I'm going crazy with this baby. He took his bottle at 9 o'clock and won't stop crying. He must have appendicitis. I'm scared out here alone at the end of the dirt road past the Seaside sign." The phone went dead. Should I go? Was it a hoax, or a trap to get narcotics from me? What if she were my wife and I was away at war? I got up and groped my way for miles around the Bay front till I found a shack at the end of a dirt road. "Jesus," I begged, "let this call be for real. I don't need trouble out here in the boondocks."

The warped door swung open at my knock, and there stood a frail childlike girl with exhaustion written on her face, bouncing a little week-old infant in her arms. She burst into tears of relief when she saw my doctor's bag. "Oh, you *did* come! No one else would—not all week. I had him here by myself because I don't know anyone since Bob left for Corrigidor. Do you know about babies?" I wanted to cry too, but I smiled and took the baby from her. I had a hunch: "Have you tried laying the baby down?" "No. Mother told me once that babies have to be held and rocked, so I've done it all week." In the corner I spotted a box with "FRESNO GRAPES" printed on the end, with a faded piece of blanket in it. I put the sobbing body down and tucked the blanket around the little bones. Almost at once he was asleep. I turned and grasped her hands: "Please promise me to come to my office tomorrow and have the nurse tell you about infant care. It's really fun when you know how." She did. And it was!

INCIDENT FIVE

My first pay-as-you-go patient was a millionairess from the 17-Mile Drive of Carmel. She gingerly smoothed her beautiful black dress as she eased her aging frame into one of my old reception room chairs opposite the second one occupied by a husky young cannery worker. In the tiny room it was hard to ignore each other. She broke the silence: "You man, just what do *you* do for a living?" I heard her query him through my open conference door.

He looked at her finery a moment and soberly answered: "I work at the egg plant, Madame." "Oh? I've heard of them. And what do you do there?" "I have charge of putting the shells on the eggs before they go in the boxes, My Dear," he replied hiding a smile. "How well you do it!" she exclaimed; "I must come and visit your factory sometime." "Yes, you do that," he said, and hid his grin behind a magazine.

I figured it was time to break up the conversation, and ushered her into my office. "Can I help you?" "Yes, young man, please call the Doctor." She was looking me over through a hand-held monicle on a gold chain unwound from an ornate little receptacle on her shoulder. "I *am* the Doctor," I blurted in surprise. "You are a cute one. Why, you're still in High School, sonny"; she smiled knowingly. "Yes, I do look young," I admitted. "You see, I started med. school at the age of four so I graduated early. Let me try to help you."

She glanced furtively around the room to be sure we were alone, and leaned so she could whisper in my ear: "Did your mother ever tell you about THE CHANGE?" I noticed a blush. "Oh yes," I assured her. "In fact she went through it beautifully, just like you are doing!" From then on we were friends: me with a patient, she with a hormone!

INCIDENT SIX

This fellow was in real pain! His dirty, smokey clothing made him look pitiful as he hobbled through the door holding his lower back. "Doc," he grunted, "I slipped on a wet stone up Carmel Valley this morning and I can't straighten up. Are you one of those Chiro fellows?

Can you help me?" Yes, I could help, but I was a Physician and Surgeon, D.O., I explained. I finally got him onto the table and corrected his sacro-iliac twist; it was beautiful to see his look of relief and amazement. "Golly, Doc, you're really good for a young fellow. Sorry I don't have a dime to pay you. Maybe I can figure something out though." I watched him through the window as he walked normally across the street below.

I had forgotten his poverty until a week later when he strode into the office with a grin and a parcel: "Here, fellow, this'll pay for the visit last week. Shot it myself yesterday and fixed it for yah. Hope your Mrs. likes it!" I was left holding the (paper) bag. In it was a hind quarter of wild boar; skin, bristles, and hoof. It was the first meat we had had since I caught the ling cod a week ago; I thanked My Provider en route home, forgetting that Maybelle was pregnant. Her first look did the trick: she disappeared into the bathrom and emerged a bit pale. But she was a trooper, besides being hungry! Somehow she made it last for six days till I could go fishing again. She reminded me that the Lord promises to supply our needs, not our tastes.

INCIDENT SEVEN

My rich "monicle lady" was back, this time carrying a tiny black poodle. "This is an emergency," she announced: "Fifi needs a treatment right away. She ran in front of a car an hour ago and her back legs won't work. You're the only doctor I will entrust her to!" "But, Mrs. M . . . , dogs go to veterinaries for their care." "Not my Fifi, young man," she retorted: "No dog doctor is going to touch her!"

Curiously, I palpated along her tiny spine: it felt broken alright, and the legs were dangling limp. "She will require Xrays in order to know what to do," I explained. "Alright, sonny, phone your hospital and I'll take her there. Be quick about it!"

I had a sudden thought: "We are fresh out of dog film at our Hospital, Mrs. M . . . , but they have two pieces left at the Animal Hospital reserved for special cases! Maybe I can talk them into taking Fifi's pictures and caring for her right there this very afternoon!" She beamed back at me as she hustled out the door. I could hear her mumbling happily something about "special film for my Fifi . . ." I knew that life for her had suddenly become worth living.

INCIDENT EIGHT

A few years later I would become known as another absent-minded professor, but the symptoms apparently started in Monterey.

The phone jolted me awake—almost 1:30 A.M. "This is the Monterey Police Station, Doc. We want to report that we just broke into your office to see why a light was on. There was a fellow in your back room with just his shorts on—claims he's a patient of yours. Says you put him under the heat lamp with the timer on and he fell asleep till we woke him up breaking down the door. Says he's Mr. Baker, and that his backache is gone and he wants to go home. Shall we hold him here for investigation? Could be a robber." I was laughing through my tears: Tell Mr. Baker I forgot all about him in the back room, and locked up and went home. Tell him, no charge for the cure, and no charge for your letting him out of the building! Give him a cup of coffee on me. Tell him that I don't think he will have any more backaches." And he didn't.

INCIDENT NINE

The opening of Fort Ord after Pearl Harbor was the signal for a mass invasion of Monterey of hordes of bartenders and prostitutes eagerly milking off the paychecks of the thousands of our country's young defenders. Within weeks Monterey counted 105 Bars and 5 recognized Red Light Houses, not to mention the score of house trailers which moved from block to block. The Army officials threw up their hands as control became ineffective, and turned the job over to the Monterey Police. That involved me. Anyone arrested for drunkenness or soliciting had to be examined and certified by the police doctor. At best the business was a sordid succession of human faults, but there was a light side with many a chuckle.

I was still sleepy early Sunday morning when I reached the Station on a drunk call. The Sargent motioned for me to use the empty Chief's Office for the sobriety test. I started filling out the voluminous forms while the Sargent brought in the drunk woman and sat her down behind me. Her speech and smell established the diagnosis without looking around at her. When I finished writing, I turned around: she was standing stark naked on her filthy pile of clothing. She grinned sickly: "Go ahead, examine me like the Sargent said." "But this is a sobriety test," I explained. "Oh H . . l, Buddy, I coulda told yah I'm stoned. When a man says "examination," I strip. Didn't know there was another kind!"

An explosion of laughter came from the doorway: there stood the whole night force crowding to see through the one-way glass. The Sargent pushed into the room: "Put 'em back on, Bessy. No business tonight." He turned to me: "Doc, meet Bessy. We thought we'd have a little fun with you tonight. She's the madam at House No. 3 on the Row. Oldest in the business. Always strips when she's alone with a man. Got syphilis in High School and it ate her brain up. Harmless now, but we put her in the tank on weekends so she'll sober up and not get hurt."

I was wishing silently that the current High School class could see what alcohol and syphilis and harlotry could do to any of them who thought it was "cute" to defy good advice by experimenting with "the boys." Maybe it was funny, but the humor was sick.

INCIDENT TEN

The phone rang at 2 A.M. beside my pillow. "Is that you, Doc? Can you drop over and see my neighbor? Remember me? You delivered my baby last month. He's looking for a "veteranary doctor." You see, he's a veteran and entitled to one free." My mind came awake with a jolt: here was a chance to play a joke on the meanest MD in town who just happened to be the official physician for veterans. He disliked me because I was "an upstart from L.A." "Let me tell you what to do," I said with a grin. "Call Dr. Martin and tell him that you need a Veterinary Doctor for a night call; and mention that I think *he* is the best." I hung up.

Sure enough: the next morning we chanced to stop at the same corner pharmacy. Without breaking stride when he saw me, he did a rightabout face and yelled in my ear as he brushed past me, "Damn you! Veterinary!" From that day on he never said ill of me: in fact, never said anything about me. The "upstart" had won.

INCIDENT ELEVEN

I was pleased and surprised when a Czech mother with three little children marched into the office one morning. She explained that she was a farmer from up the valley and was pregnant again. I was her last hope, she said, since all the other doctors refused to deliver her with her children present! She insisted that they had watched animals born, and she had gotten pregnant this time so they could see "how a baby comes out. "It is part of their training," she claimed. "They sleep with us," she volunteered. I looked them over: 2, 4, and 5 years old, a boy and two girls, hardly ready for a delivery scene! "Sorry, Mrs. Pocov, but the State law forbids little children in a sterile delivery room—for several good reasons—including your safety!" She was crest-fallen and defeated. "How will they ever learn?" she sighed, gathering her brood and heading for the elevator.

I had forgotten about her when the hospital phoned for me six months later to hurry over and deliver Mrs. Pocov who claimed to be my patient! Fortunately, she was there alone, and delivered easily without benefit of an audience. The next day she returned to her farm, explaining that the animals had to be fed and bred.

Three months later I bumped into her at a market, and asked about the baby. "He's just fine, Doctor, and growing fast" was the proud answer. "By the way," I queried, "is he still on hospital formula?" "Oh no, I switched him to goat's milk." "Did you have any trouble making the change?" I asked. "Quite a little at first," she acknowledged. "It was a restless Nanny and nearly kicked the baby's head several times while he was nursing. but it finally learned to stand still." I got the picture instantly. It still brings a chuckle.

INCIDENT TWELVE

In the Professional Building's lobby was a large directory of all the doctors' offices on the six floors. One night I was the last to leave the building and noted two fishermen still dressed in their boots and sardine-saturated shirts studying the names on the directory. Both were about 20 years old, a Mexican and a Philipino. I stopped and asked if I could be of help. They glanced at each other, sort of embarrassed, and the Mexican spoke first: "My fran' here, Man-ooh-el, he no can read." (It was obvious that he couldn't either.) "He get trouble on boat this week, Steinbeck's boat: he write books. We stop on island two days. Man-ooh-el got a trouble there. You dok-toar? Maybe you woo-man dok-toar?" They were looking at me with desperate hope.

"No, I'm not a woman doctor. But why would you men want a *woman* doctor anyway?" I asked.

Again they exchanged furtive glances. "Si, Man-ooh-el need that. My fran has a woo-man disease." His compassion was born of mutual distress! They both had a woo-man disease, and Mr. Steinbeck had ordered them off the boat till they got treatment. Two weeks later I sent them back to Steinbeck, healthier but probably no wiser. They set sail for another island that day.

INCIDENTS THIRTEEN, FOURTEEN AND FIFTEEN

My protected childhood and Christian environments before starting my medical training had ill-prepared me to understand the seamy side of life where so many patients would be living. God had to correct this; and He started by throwing me before the harsh teachers of carnal affairs. Ever since, I have been able to say (like the slap-in-the-face commercial) "I needed that!"

God showed me that not all womankind think and act as did those in my family or Wheaton. Each encounter would teach me a sad truth as I became Police Doctor for the prostitute population being booked through our town. Usually in groups of 20, they were herded by the pimps on 4-week "engagements" between Dallas, Las Vegas, Ft. Ord, and San Francisco. Inwardly they were a sorry lot; financially they were on top of the world; emotionally, they were all losers.

Marguerita I met during her heart attack. The burly Sargent met me at 11 P.M. at the waterfront House (incidentally, described colorfully in Steinbeck's Cannery Row). "Quick, Doc," he yelled as we jumped from our cars, "the Madam's got a girl dying on her hands." The waiting room was packed shoulder to shoulder with laughing drunk youngsters in uniform through whom the Sargent burrowed a tunnel for me to follow him up the stairs. Nude and ashen, she lay gasping on a dirty mattress, her heart flopping under the skinny ribs like a dying chicken. I shooed the half-dressed audience of leering faces out of the room, and administered I.V. medications.

The next week at my office she told of a frightful

childhood in a Mexican village. With a heart damaged by Rheumatic endocarditis, she had been unable to fend off the boy's gangs who used her "to learn how." At 15 she wandered north to get "Yankee doah-larr" to pay for medicines for her heart and her pelvic disease. A pimp found her first. All I could do was to refer her to the County Hospital in Salinas for proper care. I doubt that they cared: after all, there was war brewing; "so what if someone gets hurt?"

One midnight I learned about an old law on the books that every harlot had long ago memorized. It states that no officer can confine a pregnant prostitute in a jail without clinical facilities. The ancient Monterey jail had few *utilities* let alone *facilities*! The Sargent pointed to the "female tank" in the smelly basement: "We picked 'em up out of an old trailer. They both claim they are pregnant." He laughed: "Look at 'em, Doc." I did. Such woe-begone worn-out ladies of the night were unbelievable. Both in their 60's. "Of course we are pregnant! You can't hold us," they snorted, patting their flabby stomachs. Naturally, they lost that argument: they were born losers already. Satan had two voluntary prospects for his Pit!

Not often do four beautiful college girls walk into an office together; much less do they ask to be examined as a group! I gasped first in admiration, then in surprise. "We're here for medical clearance tests," the spokesman explained. "We are required to see that each other actually gets her smears taken! Aren't you the Police Doctor?" I nodded and completed the tests. "Before you leave, girls, please tell me how four gorgeous young ladies got into your racket." They were both reluctant and relieved to tell their stories, true but tragic. They were classmates at the swanky Mills College up north, all from wealthy homes.

As freshmen each had fallen madly in love with a cross-town athlete who promised marriage if "she was compatible." Within days each was discovering that her name had shown up in "little black books" available to fraternity members. Anger and disgust resulted. "We vowed to make fools of all men, right then," said shapely Doris. "Any man's a fool to pay for a girl's body. None of us could go back home and face our parents, so we're taking fools' money to pay our way through college and get a better job." "God," I said inwardly, "They could be my sisters!" Aloud I said: "Someday you'll know forgiveness and can extend it to others." They looked blankly at me; one turned as they left the room and commented: "Whoever forgives anybody?" I hoped they would learn "Who."

INCIDENT SIXTEEN

I had once read in Ecclesiastes 7:12 that "Wisdom is an asset and money is an asset; but the best part of knowledge is that wisdom giveth life to them that have it." My darling little office girl had little of either, but she was pure in heart and delighted with her salary of a dollar a day. An orphan, she was helping her Catholic grandmother meet the bills. Unwittingly she taught me some lessons about young life, and gave me some needed laughs as a dividend.

Monday morning I arrived at the office to find her already there, red-eyed from sobbing. Several slides lay next to the microscope (which she did not know how to use). I was puzzled. "Monica dear, what is wrong?" She hesitated, then broke into tears. "I'm ... I'm ... pregnant," she sobbed and collapsed in a chair. "I tried to test myself. I'm so scared, Doctor. Do you hate me for being bad? Grandma will." Her prayerbook lay open on the corner of my desk.

I smiled inwardly. "Do you know how a girl gets pregnant?" I gently asked. "Sure. Grandma warned me; if I ever sit on a boy's lap, I'll have a baby. Last night I had to sit on Joe's lap 'cause the car was full of us coming home from church. What will God do to me now?" "Oh, He'll just keep on loving you a little extra every day, honey," I promised as I held her hands. She needed a father's love right now; perhaps I could substitute. "It's time for you to learn a few things, Monica. Your Grandma loves you, but her advice was a bit old-fashioned." In a few minutes as we looked at medical illustrations about conception, she was all smiles. "Naturally, I wouldn't do *that*—not till I was married by the Priest!" she said in righteous disgust.

A year later she returned from her honeymoon and signed up for her prenatal care. I hired her to conduct some classes for the other young mothers who had "sat on boy's laps." I knew she could speak now with authority!

MIRACLE 26

It Ended With Flowers

"Whereas you know not what shall be on the
morrow. For what is your life? It is even a vapor that
appeareth for a little time, and then vanisheth away.
For ye ought to say, If the Lord will, we shall live;
and do this, or that." James 4:14, 15

Pearl Harbor was the 20th century shot heard round
the world, and it rocked Monterey. Not an American life
was left unaffected, including ours.

After Church that Sunday morning I was painting
my garage when a neighbor yelled over the fence about
the attack. Only God knew then that life for all of us
would never be the same. From that night on no light
shown along the coast; no autos could use their
headlights; no fireplace fires were lighted; total blackout
was the word: No sub was to find a target. Each block had
its civilian warden with authority to arrest violators. Most
people cooperated; they were scared!

Within weeks Monterey was a ghost town except for
soldiers and business people. Local headlines announced
"official opinions from Naval Intelligence" that indicated
Monterey would be the landing point for Japanese invaders heading here from Hawaii. Two-thirds of the
townspeople joined the mass pandomonium to get out of

gunshot somewhere in the midwest. Rows of empty houses stood silent along the streets. I investigated several of the homes of former patients who failed appointments: decaying food was still on the tables, and clothing hung abandoned in the closets. "It looks like a "rapture" has occurred," I told Maybelle, "but I fear the real one won't be this extensive!"

In their panic to leave, no one had paid any bills. The only business left alive was the florist shop: soldiers were still ordering flowers for their (one-day) weddings, and funerals and cemeteries required constant servicing. In six weeks my practice dropped to one patient a day (though the night work at the Station remained brisk). I went to work for the downstairs florist between the infrequent phone calls. I could sense that this was the end of our "training days" in beautiful Monterey where God had patiently taught us so many lessons that we would need for the future. We prayed for an answer—where next?

God said, "Start looking. I know, but you must find the place I have chosen for you." It was that simple—and that difficult.

We used long weekends to check out possibilities. I divided the State map in four likely areas, and started at Oakland. It was attractive but there was not an office available in a radius of 50 miles: every square foot under roof was appropriated by government personnel. Then we tried the Central Valley: every doctor said "Stay out—things are rough enough without sharing patients!" Next we toured the coastal towns north of Ventura: worse yet—panic and poverty. Lastly, we headed for southern California—the most heavily populated area and the least attractive to us. We worked our way from the sea coast eastward till we were in the last town inside L.A. County limits—the site of the German Prisoner-of-War Camp, named Pomona, after the Goddess of fruits and nuts! That described us! This must be it! God said, "Stop here. I have plans for you."

I pulled into a gas station with a phone booth. "May," I said, "You get two dollars of gas while I phone some doctor to ask about Pomona." I could hardly believe the yellow pages which listed the name of a former classmate just two blocks away! I drove around the block and knocked on his door. He looked at us in disbelief: "Dick and May, what are you doing here? Golly you look good. I sure wish you lived here so we could work together!" Jokingly I prodded him: "What's it worth to you, Bill, to get me to stay?" "I'll loan you a hundred dollars to cover you first month's overhead of an office and home." May and I exchanged glances: that was three times what we had in the bank after nearly three years up north. And Bill was the only one in the State who had even mentioned helping us get re-located! Two hours later we knew this was the place—though we didn't know why. Other doors had slammed closed: this one popped open!

That evening we celebrated our "Find" by dining with Bill and his vivacious wife, Bobby. We had stopped at a rail-side meat market where a pleasant lady butcher carved a huge slice of round steak from a hind quarter "saved for special people like Bill & Bobby." Neither of us knew that a year later she would be the mother of a baby boy whom Jesus would raise from the dead for the benefit of all of us! We left without even remembering her name, but Jesus had plans for us to meet again.

MIRACLE 27

The $15,000 Degree

> "Tell them to use their money to do good. They should be rich in good works and should give happily to those in need, always ready to share with others whatever God has given them. Doing this they will be storing up real treasure for themselves in heaven—it is the only safe investment for eternity." I Timothy 6:18, 19 (Living Bible).

Leaving Monterey was not all that easy. We had established many fine friendships which were painful to sever. And our "miracle" house had become a real home after the "heap o' livin'" we had experienced there in three event-packed years. The only easy part was the notifying of patients that we were leaving town: there was hardly a handful of envelopes to address and stamp. For practical purposes, Monterey was already a military and navy base: civilians were totally incidental.

The laughing matter was the way we looked as I slammed the car door to prevent the last item (bird cage with bird) from falling out. (Fibber McGee's closet was a poor second to my job of stuffing the Chevy.) I had made a baby-sized stretcher out of broomsticks and a baby blanket for Carol to sleep on while it lay perched between the front and back seats. Walter could crawl and sprawl under it on the cushion between the cartons of important incidentals needed on the southward safari. Maybelle sat in front holding a box of kitchen utensils forgotten by the moving van that pulled away a few minutes ahead of us. With a tear I shifted the gear and we waved goodbye to our good neighbors who were throwing kisses to the children. One chapter was ending. What would the next one reveal?

The answer was quick in coming! Dr. "Bill" warmly greeted us at his cottage after we left the moving van at the house we had rented by mail beside the railroad tracks, a block away. (Cheap, but comfortable, said the ad.) He was so glad to see us *really* here, he said, "But it is too bad that the hospital closed yesterday, because I had figured we could assist each other there."

I was dumbfounded. No hospital? And both of us trained for that work? He explained that the owner, an R.N., was experiencing severe menopausal instability, and had decided Friday night to "chuck the whole thing and quit listening to patients' complaints!" True, it was a small hospital, doing mostly maternity, but it was well equipped and would have served us well.

"How about office space? Did you find one for me?" I asked. "No, there's not a room in town this week, Dick, suitable for your quality of care," he replied. "You get unloaded now. Perhaps tomorrow we can find something."

In the morning we announced to the Lord that we had arrived! Now it was up to Him to find some answers. He did. Behind a door marked BOOTH BROS. I was greeted by Jack: "So you're a doctor? Looking for an office, I suppose. Not one in town, but you look ingenious. See that Beauty Shop across the street? Closed last week. Long and narrow. Outlets along the wall, and a toilet in back. Put up some wires with sheets on 'em, and you'll have four booths. Only $25 per month and I'll throw in utilities!" I had found "His" office. After all, He started in a stable—without utilities!

What God was keeping secret for the moment would become my initial reason for success. The office was only three doors from the First Baptist Church. God had arranged that the dignified and gracious secretary to its busy pastor would get suddenly ill the first morning I got my sheets strung on the wires. Her own doctor was out of town so she "tried" me, being next door. Without equipment, only by bag, I could only look wise and sound smart. "Am I really your first patient in Pomona?" she queried. "You're it, alright," I admitted, "I don't even have a money bag yet!" We both laughed.

Then God did me a favor: overnight he cured her and let her give *me* the credit. (In those days, Baptists generally believed that God blessed people *up to* the point of healing.) I was unaware during that first month afterwards that my name was becoming a "house-hold" word in the Church. God was moving sick people to call the Church for a referral to a doctor, and the secretary was sending them to me! Now I needed a hospital. Why not ask for one?

Again God whispered. "That nurse feels desperate today. Ask her to sell you the hospital!" I gasped: Not a cent in the bank; I owe Dr. Bill $100; rent, clothes, food ... etc. "Ask her today," He repeated.

I locked the office door and headed up the street. The SANBORN HOSPITAL sign was dark but I knocked. A glum R.N. answered sourly, "Yes?" "I'm Dr. Eby, here to buy your hospital!" "You're what?" she stammered. "Will you sell?" I heard myself say. "Of course if you have $17,500 cash!" Frankly, I couldn't count that high, but I again heard myself saying, "I'll be back in the morning;" and I turned and fled in panic at what I had implied to her.

Dr. Bill's office was in the Bank Building, fourth floor. I turned his knob quietly, hoping he was out and I could get off the hook. He was in. "Bill, you and I are going to buy a hospital tomorrow." "What with?" he exclaimed. "Faith," I replied. "Do you know the banker downstairs?"

My family in Pomona in 1943, living on faith and mortgages.

Mr. Stone was a beautifully sculptured banker: courteous, friendly, and stone-faced. He listened in amazement: two kids out of college ready to compete with the "establishment" at the "big hospital;" both in debt, but wanting to provide a "family medicine" hospital for "personalized care." The very ridiculousness of the proposal triggered a long-forgotten germ of pioneering in his banker's head. He shook it, and said, "Wait for me, boys."

It seemed like hours. When he returned, he was still shaking his head: "I phoned Dunn & Bradstreet in New York: somewhere they have acquired a three-year profile on you two. They say you're good risks to loan $15,000. I couldn't do that, but I will loan you $7500 if you'll secure it with all the assets you have. Maybe your nurse friend will carry the balance." She did.

From that day on Mr. Stone was our friendly banker! For the next 20 years he took a secret delight in helping us do the impossible (something a banker is not permitted normally). At heart he was a "boy" as much as we were. When he went to his reward a few years ago, the whole town became a bit poorer.

MIRACLE 28

How Do I Look?

> "Is there any sick among you? Let him call the elders
> of the church, and let them pray over him. . . . and the
> prayer of faith shall save the sick and the Lord shall
> raise him up . . ." James 5:14, 15

Why does a loving God permit pain and illness in His
children? If He is the Healer, the Great Physician, how can
He tolerate the anguish which He sees among His
creatures? (Any Christian doctor repeatedly ponders these
questions as he moves from room to room in the office or
hospital.)

This day was no exception. During the ten-mile drive
from Pomona to a hospital where my first cancer patient
was awaiting surgery, I was troubled for an answer. This
lady in her late forties was a sweet Christian soul,
reluctant to complain even when her enlarging abdomen
had become too distressing to ignore. Although she feared
cancer, she said, due to the "awful radio ads" about it, she
was sure that she did not have a malignancy. In fact,
available tests showed no more than a huge pelvic tumor
the size and shape of a pregnancy near term. Almost with
delight she accepted the scheduled operation in perfect
confidence that "her doctors would take it out" and leave

her well in a day or so! She believed God had led her to me.

I arrived at the hospital without a clear-cut answer as to why this believer and I should have met: perhaps God would somehow let me know. In the dressing room my senior surgeon warmly greeted me (because I had referred him a case?), and commented on the "huge fibroid" we were about to remove. He did not share my spiritual concerns; his goal involved being an excellent surgeon, a prominent business figure, and a successful climber in political medicine. I trusted his expertise, and so did my patient.

We looked aghast at her opened abdomen: our worst fears were confirmed. No tissues were identifiable, just a mass of red, rotten-looking friable carcinoma invading gut, bladder, and pelvic walls. Situation inoperable! Dr. W. and I looked at each other as do two surgeons faced with total defeat. (Only those thoughtless ingrates who sue doctors for money fail to realize the anguish in a doctor's heart when forced to anticipate the inevitable prognosis of death!)

Although there was no point in doing further surgery, we could not close the incision without reducing the size of the abdominal contents. Together, in silence, we literally scooped handfuls of bloody disintegrating tissue into a table-side pail until it was halfful and her pelvis was half empty! No organs were yet separately identifiable. With sick hearts Dr. W. and I closed the incision, putting the hopeless oozing mess out of sight.

I quaked inwardly enroute to the waiting room where her hope-filled family awaited a good word. What would God have me say? As usual whenever I would ask such a

question, the answer came back, "The truth, of course."
But it was not easy.

"Folks," I blurted, "she made it through surgery."
They sighed with relief. "But," I continued, "it is no credit
to us. She has invasive metastatic carcinoma; and all we
could do was to remove enough tissue to permit us to close
the incision. She is oozing internally. There is no hope,
medically speaking. Mercifully she will slip away today
before she regains consciousness. If you believe in miracles, now is the time to seek one." I had to turn and leave,
ashamed of my cracking voice. At the nurse's station I left
word to phone me when she died.

By 4:00 P.M. I had heard nothing so I drove back in
hopes of arriving in time to comfort the family. As I gently opened the door to Room Six a cheerful voice stopped
me in my tracks: "Doctor, will you please make those
nurses let me go to the bathroom!" I glanced at the room
number: yes, this was the right room; but it must be a new
patient, just admitted. I backed out and asked the charge
nurse where my patient had been sent. "Sent? We left her
in room six. Isn't she there?" Her look of fright was real.

This time I smiled as I leaned over the bed to check
the face. I had a hunch that someone's prayer had been
answered. She was very much alive! In fact, righteously
indignant about her siderails being up! "Doctor," she
reminded me, "You said I could go home as soon as I was
well enough. I suppose there are stitches under my bandage, but I can come back to have them out next week. I'll
wait till morning if you insist; that will give time for the
family to clean up the house before I get home!" She
smiled at her clever intrigue in getting out of doing
housework herself.

Four days later I finally agreed to release her, since

she was practically directing hospital traffic by then! Her family told me how their Brethren Church friends had simply *prayed* for her recovery after surgery, and *expected* it to happen. No great deal; simply ask and it shall be done unto you, they said! I was more excited than they; this was my first case of miracle healing in a hospital (it would not be the last, praise God).

About fifteen years later I casually dropped around to congratulate the president of a new Pomona banking center at its open house. He escorted me to the punch bowl where a familiar face greeted me with, "Hello, Doctor, how have you been?" No healthier looking hostess could I have imagined! "You know, Doc, I have never had a sick moment since you cured me. I knew you would fix me up the moment I laid eyes on you. Never had to come back to see you. How do I look?" This time she was ministering to me!

Naturally, I disclaimed any credit. Only Jesus knows how many lives were changed through her healing. My surgeon friend became a missionary in Ecuador to everyone's surprise! Several in the little church experienced "a closer walk." I became better prepared for the next miracle a week later. In fact, I began to realize that there is no healing possible apart from God's laws, whether they be natural (as we know them) or supernatural (as we have yet to learn them). That is a "heavy lesson": it takes years to sink through a doctor's skull and take root as "faith"!

MIRACLE 29

I Never Give Up

"I am the good shepherd and know my sheep, and am known of them." John 10:14

In truth the birth of a baby is a miracle so commonplace after centuries of reproduction that it merits little more than an obscure paragraph in a neighborhood newspaper. Childbirth nevertheless is a headline in heaven! (Not even the highest angel in the seventh heaven can aspire to experience parenthood, nor relish the gift of motherhood.) Only a personal God could have engineered the exquisite chemistry and the physics needed to accomplish the fantastic journey from cramp to cradle.

Time after time the Creator has used childbirth to teach a lesson about power, justice, or mercy. Although His laws of life are the same now as when He gave them to Adam and later to Moses, yet they can be adjusted to fit *special* needs. When this happens, we mortals call it a *miracle* since we have no comprehension of divine thought processes. Only God's power can effect such molecular or spiritual readjustments. And each such occasion is meant to demonstrate His justice or mercy. The enablement He uses is called AGAPE, a beautiful word for His kind of LOVE.

I shall never forget how He handled a newborn

problem early in my practice. He wanted me to learn who is *really* the obstetrician on each case!

It had been a long night for the mother and me. She was a fine, hardworking butcher at a meat market in town, who had started labor after a tiring day behind the counter. The sun had just come up when her husky eight-pound boy finally arrived with a scream of disgust at discovering what a bewildering world of light and air he had entered. His wails were only matched by the squeals of delight from his tired but adoring mother. He was a beauty, and she loved him just as he was. The waiting family scurried to the phones to share their joy, as I changed clothes to drive to a neighboring town to deliver another mother there.

A half hour later the phone on the delivery room wall rang to notify me to rush back to Pomona; the new baby had suddenly stopped breathing just a minute before, and the nurse could not detect any life. I gasped, and ordered her to call the Resuscitator Squad from the Fire Department to work on the body until I could complete my work and drive back. (In those war years our only emergency resources were the police and firemen.) As I finished this delivery, my mind was racing to review every possible reason why a healthy baby would stop breathing. None emerged.

Driving back seemed twice as far, and my watch revealed 50 minutes since the little boy had first stopped breathing. En route I implored Jesus to rush ahead and revive the body; it was all I could do. The scene was somber as I burst through the nursery door: uniforms huddled over the bassinet and only the click-click of the respirator broke the silence. The firemen shook their heads: "He was dead when we arrived a half-hour ago,

Doc. We stayed till you could get here. The nurse said to."
I quickly checked for a sign of life. None at all. Already the little body was grey and cold, gone.

"Thank you. You may leave now," I whispered to the squad. The nurse turned away to hide a tear, and I laid my hand on the cold head. "Dear Jesus," I prayed, "He was so loved down here! Won't you give him back to us? His mother needs him, just like my mother needed me." What more could I say?

I felt and heard the sudden cough at the same time! The body seemed to convulse. I opened my eyes and the nurse shouted "Look!" A fireman jumped through the doorway and shouted, "I'll be damned!" The baby coughed and screamed. He turned pink and started shivering like he had just returned from a cold place. I could say nothing; just stand and enjoy the miracle of answered prayer.

Naturally, the mother wondered why there had been so long a delay in bringing her newborn to her room. I explained that he had a "little trouble" at first getting used to earth-living, but God had shown him how, and he was very happy now. I was certainly not going to frighten her mother's heart with the whole story, especially since God had things under control.

The medical books say that eight minutes without breathing is fatal for infant brain tissue. Even partial anoxia can cause a "vegetable" type of deterioration. En route home that evening I asked for one more miracle: "Please, Jesus, give that baby a new brain undamaged and unhampered by these long minutes of death!" He did. Sixteen years later the local Progress-Bulletin carried the story of the fine football captain at Pomona High: he was "our" baby—scholastically and physically a winner!

There is no doubt about it: Jesus does things well!

MIRACLE 30

Victories and Defeats

"Bow down thine ear, Oh Lord, near me, for I am poor and needy. Be merciful unto me, O Lord, for I cry unto Thee daily. Show me a token for good; that they who hate me may see it, and be ashamed; because thou, Lord, hast helped me, and comforted me." Psalm 86:1, 3, 17

Despite attacks from "flesh and blood" as well as "principalities and powers," the little hospital survived! Maybelle and I prayed so hard that our plunge into the hospital "business" would bring blessing to the patients who trusted the care of our colleagues and myself who would support it. God listened, taught lessons, then gave answers.

Bill and I were so excited when the escrow officer phoned us to pick up the key to OUR hospital that we arrived there in a mental fog of expectancy. We were not ready for the let-down! From room to room we searched for the beds and equipment which were missing. The place had been stripped: no surgery table or supplies, no stands, no lamps, not even bedding. Only three broken beds and exposed pipes where the autoclaves had been removed. The nurse had recognized our youthful ignorance, discovered that we had not included the "chattel" (a new word to us) in the escrow, and had sold off everything to a neighboring hospital. We were crushed!

That night I cried. "Surely, Jesus, You have a reason," I sobbed. "All our money is gone, and we have a useless building. You knew our needs. TELL us what to do next!" He already had the answer for us (as He always does) but He took six weeks to test our faith. Then a tired young man asked my receptionist to see me. "What about?" she naturally asked. "Just to get acquainted, I guess," he stated with a shrug.

He told me his story of answering an ad for a job at an L.A. surgical supply company a week ago, and of the long drive here from Ohio. From the stop at the intersection in front of the church he spotted my office sign and decided to stop for some reason "and make a Pomona contact" to help get the job in L.A. If I could perchance say that I would buy from him (if he were hired), he might have a talking point!

"I'll level with you," I replied. "All I need is equipment to outfit a small hospital, and I know you don't have that, much less for a song!"

His face paled, "I can't believe it. Two days ago I stopped in Utah at a small Mormon hospital and met the doctor as he was locking the door. 'If you're a salesman, he laughed, 'sell this one! This is my last day in my hospital. I'm old, and the war has put me out of business. Get me $500 and you can carry off everything except the building!' He handed me a business card, and said he would wait for my call. He acted like I would meet someone who wanted to buy the contents of his 20-bed hospital! Can you beat that?"

No, I couldn't. But two phone calls later (one to Utah

and one to Bill) and I knew that the *impossible* was oc-curing. The next morning in a rented truck Bill and the unemployed salesman were en route to Utah; a week later we were installing the essential ingredients to get started—everything except mattresses and linens. I asked God how He expected us to find those items—and the phone rang from Los Angeles. "This is the Belvedere Hospital calling. We closed two weeks ago and are trying to sell off the remaining items today. Your classmate, Dr. Allison, told us you were opening in Pomona. By any chance could you use some linens and mattresses? We have a large truck-load you can have for $50."

Bill got back in the truck and headed for Los Angeles. We all ate beans for a month, and fasted on weekends, but our hospital opened on schedule.

There is no doubt that faith appears as foolishness to skeptical on-lookers. When we admitted our first mother in labor at 1:00 A.M. on October 15, 1943 it appeared ridiculous. Only Bill, the mother and I knew it would work out. With a pressure cooker to sterilize gloves and instruments, and a home-delivery pack borrowed from a lady doctor, Bill set up the delivery room. I phoned a prac-tical nurse who was working as a fry cook but wanted back into hospital routines: "Any chance, Louise, that you could get up and come over to help out? You'll have to get meals too, until I find a cook in the morning!" She was there in a few minutes. With a squalling baby boy, a happy mother, three beds, one nurse, and an old Kenmore washing machine, we had launched our hospital into the unknown. Only God could make it work: He did.

Within a year Bill and I could not handle the business affairs after hours as we had tried at first, and I looked for a business manager. Our high-school-aged baby-sitter suggested one evening that she wanted us to meet her mother who was working as a mechanic at the Fairgrounds Prisoner Base up the street, so we drove up to the gate and Mary Lou got us past the guard. A row of drab olive Army trucks lined the entrance, and from under one of them protruded a pair of ankles shod in heavy boots.

Mary Lou tugged on them with a cheery "Hi, Ma. Come out and see Doc and May!" There emerged a slender oily green-clad figure with the sweetest smile and voice imaginable! "Meet my mother, Mrs. Dorothea Miller."

Obviously embarrassed at a first meeting in such circumstances, her gracious manner indicated her expertise in some other field. "Yes," she admitted, "I am just trying to make ends meet at this job. For years I have managed a 200-room resort in the Saranacs by the Hudson, but it closed when the war started. Do you need a hospital manager by any chance?" "No, not really," I ventured. "You see I just found one!" (For the next 25 years when friends asked me how to find someone as excellent as my business manager, I directed them to look under any disabled army truck with ankles protruding! It had worked for me.)

The answers to prayer in the following 35 years at the hospital would consume books. There were always unseen needs to be met—and they were always supplied in the nick of time. Each time we needed to build a new wing, it meant borrowing funds because our policy of maintaining the lowest rates in the county made no profit (but helped a host of friends). Each time Mr. Stone swallowed hard and signed a new loan: $55,000, $85,000, $165,000, and $350,000. Each time it was paid off before maturity, and the bankers asked "How?" We knew: God and hard work and devoted patients.

We treasure several memories of "those good old days"—good because people helped one another. Time after time the overtaxed kitchen stoves would "die" in the midst of preparing meals, and the neighbors would finish cooking the diets for us—and sometimes add a goodie. The old Maytag washing machine would groan to a halt from an overload of diapers or bedding, and the doctors' wives would lug the wet laundry home and finish the job! During the war no food stamps or other ration stamps were issued to the hospital (it was not a "person"); but each patient would bring needed toilet paper, soap or bread or hamburger to supply their needs for the few days in bed. When the roof leaked, a sympathetic contractor "borrowed" roofing from his subdivision to keep the patients dry. When we needed an emergency heated bassinet, a chicken hatchery owner designed and built a baby-sized box with a chicken thermostat which worked fine for ten years until commercial models were available! When the building needed a paint job, the doctors would show up on Saturday in overalls and work till they were needed in maternity or surgery. Seldom was anything stolen or defaced: those were the good old days for sure!

Not all was roses. When we applied for a permit to build a new surgery, we stirred up a hornet's nest at an adjoining hospital which feared competition. Quietly the lay Planning Commissioners were replaced with angry doctors who voted at a secret session to require any new surgery built in town to have an 18-inch thick steel reinforced concrete ceiling (like a freeway overpass). No contractor was set up with forms for this type of unique construction, and they knew it. I could not fight city hall (though I tried for six months) so I had a Los Angeles firm design and build special forms, transport them to Pomona and show the local masonry workers how to use them. It took six months and thousands of extra dollars, plus putting down a picket line that was thrown around the hospital by a union official who objected to "unorthodox construction practices." I prayed for help!

You wouldn't believe how He answered me: the official's wife became pregnant, insisted that she come to me for care, and badgered her husband till he called off the strikers! To top it off, when the surgery wing was completed it was inspected and found to be the only one in the state which conformed to emergency "fall-out regulations" adopted after the scare over the Pacific nuclear bomb tests of the late fifties. For laughs, the old Civilian Defense Stickers have been preserved to this day!

If the babies who have been born in this little hospital had located in one town, it would now number over 21,000, many of whom would be parents themselves. And the statistical miracle can be credited to a Divine Overseer: only two mothers in all those years died after childbirth at the hospital—both from medical causes. As is true of all healing, it is evidence of His goodness to His children on earth.

MIRACLE 31

In My Father's House

"For we know that when this tent we live in now is taken down . . . when we die and leave these bodies . . . we will have wonderful new bodies in Heaven, homes that will be ours for evermore, made for us by God Himself, without human hands." II Corinthians 5:1 (Living Bible)

I shall never know why I had always looked forward with excessive eagerness to my 60th birthday. After all, 59 birthday cakes were more than enough! God had already led me through so many valleys and up steep hills that no further experiences seemed possible.

And now we were back in Pomona after five years of absence in the Midwest where I had tried futilely to give my profession the accumulated years of knowledge and experience needed to strengthen weak areas in our political and academic ranks. I honestly believe that I accomplished many goals, but they were not appreciated then, and God seemed to be making us increasingly restless for a return to our family and grandchildren. My hospital in Pomona was still where my heart lay, and now I was 60!

Maybelle "threw a party"; the best, the biggest, the most delightful. My Indian Museum served as a focal point for the interchange of information and insight into

God's only true Americans whose chants and legends reveal that they, too, once knew Him but got lost in their wilderness and turned to idols, just as all the other colors of skin have done. I pointed out that God loves them too: His permitted persecutions will someday be counterbalanced by added blessings. In Chicago twenty days later I unexpectedly learned why my spirit had longed for a 60th birthday: God had been preparing me for the greatest gift He could wrap for me—one that I could appreciate only after learning earth's pains and trials—a moment in Paradise! A day at Home! His Peace!

My account and experience would be questionable were it not for a scriptural parallel. I found in God's Word the account by St. Paul of his trip to Paradise in the third Heaven. After being stoned to death in Lystra by the furious mob who resented his ministry and miracles, Paul was snatched from his broken body up into Paradise before being replaced into the repaired frame a few minutes later. Listen to his report: "Fourteen years ago I was taken up to Heaven for a visit. Don't ask me whether my body was there or just my Spirit, for I don't know; only God can answer that . . . There I was in Paradise, and heard things so astounding that they are beyond man's power to describe or put in words. . . . That experience is something worth bragging about, but I am not going to do it" II Corinthians 12:2-5 (Living Bible).

Please note: Paul had been cautioned not to reveal (prematurely) the earth-shaking, tradition-shattering revelations given to him there by Jesus. Never previously had God revealed the unsearchable "unutterable" riches of the "joint-heirship" with Jesus provided for Jew and Gentile alike by way of the Cross and Resurrection. Paul was being prepared by these heavenly unveilings of

Divine mysteries in order to write epistles during the long silent prison years. These "love letters" were to be God's final and complete explanation of His outpoured love to man.

No small wonder that Paul, as great a saint as was ever gifted by God, had to be restrained from the human urge to boast! Three times God refused Paul's fervent request to be released from Satan's demon of torment lest his urge to boast should surface. Those pelting stones had obviously broken his skull bones, ribs, and extremities; muscles had been crushed, and organs contused. When Jesus ordered the Spirit back into that broken body, the scar tissue and bony calluses remained as "a thorn in the flesh" to taunt and haunt his years of aching travel and clammy imprisonment.

To the glory of his Lord, fourteen years later, he victoriously wrote: "I take pleasure in *infirmities*, in necessities, in reproaches, in persecutions, in *distresses* for Christ's sake; for when I am weak, then am I strong." Because Paul exercised his own mustard seed of faith by *believing* Jesus, he could testify of this truth: "My grace is sufficient for thee: for My strength is made perfect in weakness" II Corinthians 12:10, 9.

PETITION FROM PARADISE

I was suddenly embarked upon the most "unutterable" indescribable heavenly moment of life-after-life which any Christian can be permitted. Because Jesus has since ordered me to "Tell them, tell them, tell them," I am attempting herein to share the most personal, the most spiritually resplendent, and most ecstatically moving observations which I will ever know until that great moment when we shall meet the King of Kings in the air! Only the Spirit of God, our constant Comforter and Instructor, can make my human words meaningful—and then only to Christians.

My prayer is constantly that you unbelievers who read these pages will be convinced that God's Word and promises and heaven are really real; that you will accept His free gift of Love and Life—right now. In a moment from now it may be too late. A fatal "coronary" or accident may give you *no* time for a decision tomorrow! Ask yourself "How can *I* neglect *so great salvation* freely offered by my personal Redeemer?" Silly, isn't it, to reject *any* love, especially God's, any longer?

PLUNGE INTO PARADISE

Maybelle has described for me the day's activities preceding my unscheduled visit to Paradise (the reception room to Heaven). She has told me, since my memory of that day was mercifully erased, that we were busily sorting and packing into cartons various personal effects at the Chicago home of her departed aunt and late mother. My job was to load disposables from the second and third floors, and throw the cartons to the ground below the second storey wooden balcony. A neighbor boy would take them to the dump.

A hollow crunching sound suddenly froze Maybelle in her tracks! She had an instant flashback of a similar sickening sound years ago in front of Marshall-Field's Department store in the Loop when a girl's body had plummeted at her feet from thirteen storeys up. She says that without that sickening memory she would have continued her rummaging through the closet, assuming that it was some street noise from passing traffic. (She believes that God had positioned her at that store-front long ago in anticipation of her role in this day's events.) Instead, she dashed to the balcony, noted the missing railing, and gazed down in horror at my bloody, muddy body beside the broken sidewalk. The termite-eaten railing lay across the body.

Her anguished scream alerted a neighbor lady who "happened" to have the ambulance phone number handy. Her black housekeeper "happened" to be there that day, and phoned her church's prayer-chain. (Within minutes God had things organized!)

Only recently has Maybelle been able to describe the scene she encountered upon rushing downstairs and out the back door. (The night after the accident she had prayed to be relieved of the nightmarish memory, and for four years God had mercifully erased the details. Recently she has prayed that the details be restored so that she could testify more accurately as we speak here and there.)

Quickly noting the broken railing and broken cement slab, she saw the body lying some five yards away, head-down in a pool of mud and blood, with the feet hanging in thick hedgebushes beside the sidewalk. The bloody skull was exposed with the scalp torn down over each ear. The body was already grey-white and the blood had quit flowing.

She instinctively screamed in anguish and bent to check for pulse or breath. Neither. The body was stiffly contorted, and the huge pool of bloody mud around the scalped skull spelled death. Through the parted lids she noted the dilated lifeless pupils staring fixedly. For a while she stood frozen in shock; only her mind was active as it registered her plight: "God, my Dick is dead. Help me, Lord!"

Her trance was broken by the two ambulance attendants rushing past her to check the body. They returned to the vehicle for a board stretcher and in no apparent hurry lifted the body from the bushes onto the hard surface stretcher and then out to the street and into the car. Maybelle ran through the house, grabbed her purse with identification papers, and climbed in beside the body. She noted that neither paramedic seemed in a hurry as they drove away toward the nearest trauma center hospital: no need to hurry with a d.o.a. aboard, she realized.

Yet she was still believing for a miracle. "God," she implored, "get down here right now. I need you. Don't let Dick die. I need him." Her fists pounded wildly on the dash board to emphasize her anguish.

"Please, lady, don't ruin our car," implored the attendant as he tried to comfort her. He rechecked the body and said something to the driver. Maybelle remembers that the red lights and siren suddenly went on, and the accelerator seemed to go wide open. "Has God answered my prayer?" she wondered.

THE SIGHTS OF PARADISE

"Absent from the body; present with the Lord."

In the twinkling of an eye Jesus took me out of this world. I can not adequately describe the astonishment, the amazement, the sheer shock of this event. One moment in suburban Chicago, the next moment in suburban Heaven. One moment in the miserable humidity of a midwest city, the next moment in the most exquisite place "prepared for you, that where I am ye may be also." One moment with a flesh-restricted mind, the next moment with a heaven-released mind whose speed of function was that of light!

My initial gasp ("Dick, you're dead") was as quickly followed by an overwhelming sence of Peace—peace which passeth earthly understanding—peace so complete that I instantly knew it was the promised gift of the Spirit from our Lord. I had no memory about my life on earth at this time. I was enjoying a heavenly "body"; I was totally me. Aside from the complete absence of pain and the total presence of peace (neither of which I had ever known on earth), I looked like me, felt like me, reacted like me. I was me. I simply suddenly had shed the old body and was now living anew in this fantastic cloud-like body!

Being a physician, my first instinct was to inspect my new body, and I instantly admired it! It was mine alright. After 60 years in the old one it was easy to see that the new body was me. (I am sure that God included in this entire heavenly experience only those things which would be specifically meaningful to me, for proof and edification. He would give a different set of revelations to someone with a different background.) I was the same size, the same shape, as the person I had seen in the mirror for years. I was clothed in a translucent flowing gown, pure white, but transparent to my gaze. In amazement I could see through my body and note the gorgeously white flowers behind and beneath me. This seemed perfectly normal, yet thrillingly novel.

All this time I was instinctively aware that the Lord of Lords was everywhere about this place, though I did not see Him. Instantly the sense of timelessness made all hurry foolish, so I resumed my anatomy lesson, knowing that He would appear in His own time. It all seemed so normal in this fantastic anteroom to Heaven.

My feet were easy to see. No bifocals needed. I had instantly noted that my eyes were unlimited in range of vision; ten inches or ten miles—the focus was sharp and clear. ("We shall mount up as eagles," said King David—he was alluding to their pinpoint eyesight perhaps!) There were no bones or vessels or organs. No blood. I noted the absence of genitals. (How unneeded when in Heaven there is no marriage nor childbearing—His Body of believers being already completed!) The abdomen and chest were organless and transparent to my gaze, though translucent to my peripheral vision. Again my mind which worked here in heaven with electric-like speed answered my unspoken query: they are not needed; Jesus is the Life here. His is the needed energy. There was no air to breathe, no blood to pump, no food to digest nor eliminate. This was not a carnal body of organs, mortal and temporary!

My gaze riveted upon the exquisite valley in which I found myself. Forests of symmetrical trees unlike anything on earth covered the foothills on each side. I could see each branch and "leaf"—not a brown spot or dead leaf in the forest. ("No death there" includes the vegetation!) Each tree, tall and graceful, was a duplicate of the others: perfect, unblemished. They resembled somewhat the tall arbor vitae cedars of North America, but I could not identify them. The valley floor was gorgeous. Stately grasses, each blade perfect and erect, were interspersed with ultra-white, four petalled flowers on stems two feet tall, with a touch of gold at the centers. Each was totally alike! (No two earthly flowers can be identical, nor is anything else since the Genesis curse.)

Having been an amateur botanist as a schoolboy, I immediately decided to pick a bouquet. To my amazement the unexpected happened. My thought (to stoop and pick flowers) became the act! Here in Paradise I discovered that there is no time lag between thought and act. A word, spoken or thought, became fact! (I instantly realized how the heavens and earth were so quickly made from nothing that appeared: God had simply *thought* what He wanted, and there it was. No sluggish man-invented committees were involved.)

I found my hand containing a bouquet of identical blossoms. Their whiteness was exciting. I almost had time to ask myself "why so white" when the answer was already given! "On earth you saw only white light which combined the color spectrum of the sun. Here we have the light of the SON!" My excitement was too great to describe in words: of course, I thought, He is the light of the world . . . in the new Heavens no sun or moon will be needed! Then I sensed a strange new feel to the stems—no moisture! I felt them carefully. Delicately smooth, yet nothing like earthly stems with their cellular watery content. Before I could ask, again I had an answer: earthly water is hydrogen and oxygen for temporary life support; here Jesus is the Living Water. In His presence nothing dies. No need for oxygen and hydrogen. I instinctively looked behind me where I had been standing on dozens of blooms. Not one was bent or bruised. Then I watched my feet as I walked a few more steps upon the grass and flowers; they stood upright inside my feet and legs! We simply passed through one another. (My Lord had passed through closed doors and a heavy stone over the tomb centuries ago—with the same kind of body!)

The illumination fascinated me—not a shadow anywhere. There was no single light source as on earth. I realized that everything seemed to produce its own light. Again the answer coincided with by query: the Heavens declare the glory of God; know ye not that His is the Honor, and Glory, and POWER? He *is* the Light of the world!

THE SOUNDS OF PARADISE

I stood overwhelmed with the sights of Paradise. God had shown me incontroversial evidence of His planning and preparing a place just for me, as He had promised. But He had more—it was music.

All this "time" (since there was no sun, there was actually no time reference) I had been aware of the most beautiful, melodious, angelic background music that the ear of man can perceive. I was now ready to concentrate on it. It was truly a new song, such as St. John must have heard from Patmos. Not instrumental, not vocal, not mathematical, not earthly. It originated from no one point—neither from the sky nor the ground. Just as was true of the light, the music emerged apparently from everything and every place. It had no beat—was neither major or minor—and had no tempo. (In eternity, how could it have "time"?) No earthly adjectives describe its angelic quality. Poets have said "music of the spheres." God has said, "A new song will I give them." I heard it—it had to be His composition—every note. Hallelujah! Music by Jesus. No wonder the cherubims and seraphims and multitudes sing around His throne!

THE PERFUME OF PARADISE

I was not prepared for the sweetest revelation of all: the all-pervading aroma of heaven. No one on earth, minister or Bible teacher, had mentioned to me this heady perfume! Like the sight and the sounds, it was everywhere. I bent again and smelled the flowers—yes it was there. The grasses also. The air was just the same. A perfume so exotic, so refreshing, so superior, that it was fit only for a King! Even the special formula given by Jehovah to his priests in the wilderness could not have matched this "sweet savor." Earthly ingredients would fall short of perfection. I simply stood quietly and let it bathe my being.

No answer was given my query about it in Paradise. This time Jesus waited till I was back on earth. "Search the scriptures," the Spirit advised me. "In them you will find wisdom." From Genesis and Leviticus through the books to Revelation He has told about His love of sweet smelling savors, His appreciation of the sacrifices of His worshipers, His demands for certain incense in Tabernacle worship, and finally His supreme joy in the prayers of His saints. He has preserved and mixed all these together, we are told, bottled them in golden urns, and readied them for opening before the Throne of His Lamb, Who alone is Worthy to savor their divine fragrance (Revelation 5:8)! "This is My Son in Whom I am well pleased."

I was allowed to share God's supreme perfume. Never can I be the same again. Just to realize that it is but one of the unsearchable joys prepared for all His joint-heirs to share in eternity is too infinite a gift to envision as ours. And it awaits whosoever will come to Jesus! He said it; I believe it. He prepared it; I accept it.

THE PASSING OF PARADISE

Fortunately for me, Jesus elected not to show me more of the heavenly wonders that day. I could not have coped with another revelation. This entire experience away from earth had taken only minutes, or maybe hours. Records are incomplete. It does not matter. God's purpose in taking me there and sending me back will be accomplished through His Spirit, Hallelujah! He was hearing the *prayers* of uncounted intercessors, unknown to me, as I surveyed His heavenly wonders that day. Because of them He decided to put me back on earth. He had promised that fervent prayers would avail much, and He never lies.

As I looked down the long beautiful valley with its straight and narrow path parting the flowers, I decided to find my wife and share this unbelievable peace and joy. It seemed only natural that she must have died also, since marriage had made the twain one. Instantly again I found myself going down the path, effortless, weightless, and confident. As a bend in the valley floor approached, I heard her distant voice calling "Richard, Richard . . ." As the voice grew louder, the valley grew dimmer, and the light went out. My mind stopped working and all was silent and black. Later I would realize that I was back on earth where the prayers of many had been answered for my return! And the next day I would hear Jesus speak to me on the fourth floor.

MIRACLE 32

My Peace I Give

"As for me, I will behold Thy face in righteousness: I shall be satisfied, when I awake, with Thy likeness."
Psalm 17:15

The total blackness of my unconscious mind, after the glorious light of heaven, slowly crept away hours later. Lying in the fog-like penumbra of returning consciousness I was shocked to find myself spread-eagled in Intensive Care with intravenous tubing and electrical wiring stuck in me here and there! I had no idea what had happened. I tried to move and found myself paralyzed from neck to hips. The eyes and toes could be moved slightly. My body was numb. I could not tell whether I was breathing or whether the heart was beating.

Through the fog there materialized above me a two-headed face, out of focus, surmounting a Roman collar. I then realized that my eyeballs were at different levels and that my head was encased in a helmet-type bandage. As a doctor I knew what this meant: somehow my skull had been split apart enough to shift the eyesockets; that would explain the lack of feeling and motion. But why was I alive?

I summoned every ounce of energy to form some

words: "You must be a Father," I whispered; "What are you doing?"

"Yes, I am the Chaplain," I heard him say. "I am giving you the rites of the Church." I could note his right hand shaking something over my limp body. "Thank you so much, Father; can you use Protestant water?" I heard myself say. He straightened up and chuckled, both in relief and surprise. "Doctor, you might just make it! I'll go and light a candle for you in the Chapel." "Please make it Baptist tallow, Father," I said with an attempted smile. He broke step and turned back to my bed. I could see that he was very young, and quite frightened at hearing a voice from a "dead man." The two heads bent over me and he tried to laugh: "You will live alright, I can see that," he commented as the heads slowly shook in disbelief. "Of course," I murmured, "I just came back from Heaven." His face(s) turned white and he hurried from the room. I realized that he thought his holy water had done its work; that would shock any young priest at his first sprinkling!

(Daily he returned to reassure himself that I was not a ghost. It was beautiful to see how God was using me to prove to a young chaplain that miracles can occur.)

The next I remember I was talking to a little nurse assigned to the death-watch during the night. I was distracting my mind from the agony of my pain by urging her to accept my Jesus as a real person in her life. Working with the sick and dying had hardened her heart against a "cruel God." I sensed Satan's victory; she had believed his lies and distortions. I told her how Satan is the author of sickness and death; that Jesus is the author of healing and life. In the darkness of the hot July night I was praying for a miracle of salvation in her heart.

Suddenly the room lit up. I moved my eyes toward the source: out of the plaster where the ceiling met the walls was emerging the most gorgeously sculptured cloud of "milk-glass" texture, self-illuminated! I whispered to the nurse, "Do you see anything strange in the room?" She shook her head. I lay astounded.

The Cloud was smoothly formed of rounded billows, four feet long and half as wide. "It" detached from the plaster and hung beautifully in space. Then it spoke! And the voice was Jesus! Sovereign, regal, loving, authoritative, sweet, winsome, meek, powerful! All rolled in one.

"MY PEACE I GIVE UNTO YOU!"

Startled, I again asked the nurse if she heard anything. She hadn't. Again He spoke:

"WITH YOUR HANDS YOU WILL HEAL."

I glanced sideways at them: white, bloodless, useless. Peace? I was tortured with pain in every twisted joint and tissue, and couldn't move to relieve it.

I blurted out: "You must be kidding!" This time the nurse was startled: "What do you mean, Doctor?" "Nothing," I assured her. Certainly I was not about to tell her that I was talking to a cloud!

I looked up again and He repeated His promise: "My peace I give unto you. . . . With your hands you will heal." I could see the Cloud receding majestically through the plaster, and realized that for those moments my eyesight had been 20/20. I looked back toward the nurse and fell asleep. He had given me His Peace! Another miracle.

The next morning I learned that Maybelle, also, had slept in perfect peace after casting her anguish upon the Lord. Early in the morning she had come to the hospital (having been told previously that death would take me by then). On the pillow beside my shaved head she noted the huge caputaline bandage which had dislodged during my rest, and in sudden concern she rolled my head toward her. A miracle: the lacerated scalp, from eyelid to occiput, was healed. The 180-plus stitches lay unneeded. The jagged red lines were firmly closed, and there was color in my face!

Word must have spread: around noon the surgeon appeared: "Don't get false hopes, Doc! There is no way to avoid being a vegetable. Your brain tissue yesterday was jelly where we saw it exposed. You had no blood left, so we couldn't transfuse you—the law, you know: "don't waste blood on a corpse." We wanted to do the autopsy before signing you out but we didn't have permission. We sewed the scalp back to save the mortician that job: 40 cents a stitch, you know." He smiled to release the tension he felt. "I don't know why you're still here. It beats me."

"*I* know. Jesus told me I would live!" He shook his head, "Brain injuries do funny things; you know that. Every now and then a patient talks out of his head about something religious happening. Of course we know that science knows better." He shook my hand in a farewell gesture. Obviously he hated hopeless situations and was glad to leave. He had written me off and was headed for a more favorable mission of mercy. I didn't see him again.

MIRACLE 33

Having Done All, Stand

"And the spirit entered into me when He spoke unto me, and set me upon my feet . . ." Ezekiel 2:2

I sensed a sudden change in the nursing staff. The first day I was treated with skillful neglect since they were busy with patients who would live. The second day a wave of awe and fear took over: they were scared. How do you nurse a miracle? How do you handle a bloodless vegetable? Answer: you transfer him to another floor. Besides, there was no longer room for the dozens of flower arrangements.

Miserable as I was from the terrible heat (no air-conditioning in the July weather), I was delighted to get rid of the unneeded monitor wiring and I.V. tubing. Besides, God said I would live, and that meant walking. I wanted to test His promise. That night when the nurse had left, I asked Maybelle to help me off the bed! (Being the head of the house, I convinced her it was her duty!) Sure enough, God had given me back my balance and my leg muscles; I paraded around the room, to the lavatory and back. With my glasses setting at an angle I could focus fairly well.

In the morning the nurse cheerfully predicted that I

could get out of bed in a week. "Thanks, Honey," I grinned. "I was up last night." She nearly fainted.

My son and daughter had flown immediately to Chicago from California when they had been phoned of my death. The mortician's limousine had picked them up at the airport and brought them directly to the hospital expecting to join their mother in grief. Imagine our joy to be able to praise together! I can tell them now, as then, that there is no death for His children—only a call to come home!

And speaking of home—after these four days I wanted to be home again: if I were not permitted to stay in the heavenly one, at least in the earthly one! We asked the Department Chief about returning to California: "Oh yes; we'll be glad to get you out of here," he replied with too much eagerness to conceal. (He wanted no more of this miracle business: it didn't look scientific on the hospital chart.)

It took three days to arrange airplane transportation. We learned that only one airline was chartered to handle stretcher cases, and that the Plumbers Union had the contract to unscrew the regular seats and replace them with a pipe-framework to hold the "victim." They would only work during daytime hours so it meant dovetailing their work schedule with plane take-offs. We prayed for Divine assistance; but the Union won, and we waited day after day. When we touched down finally at Los Angeles International, even the hot ambulance (that wasn't allowed onto the field) looked heavenly as it waited at the curb! Once in the hospital room furnished by my late father I fell asleep, secure that my heavenly Father would take over my future as He had done for my Dad.

I awoke to hear a cheerful and familiar voice.

Another miracle, so it seemed. There stood my colleague, Dr. Lay, a lady doctor skilled in cranial manipulation to align distortions in the head bones. She had been at a conference in Chicago the day before, had heard of my injury, and took the next plane to Pomona. "Here I am, Dick. Let's get this head on straight!" she quipped as she moved the bed to reach my head. "Oh my God. I didn't know it was this bad," she exclaimed, noting the two halves out of line. "They sewed the scalp over the skull without putting it back together! How do you function at all?

"God sent me back to teach several lessons about body functions. He left a few parts unrepaired for you to fix!"

"Could be. Never saw the likes before. But here goes." She gently held the crooked head and began molding it back toward normal. In an hour my eyes began to focus; the lopsided jaw would close; the ears were almost level; and the ugly ridge along the skull was disappearing as the sutures slid together. After a few more treatments the structure of the head was nearly restored, and functions were improving daily. God had trained her hands over the years just for this challenge: so it seemed to me, and I still believe it.

In order to answer our prayers or do a miracle God prepares us long in advance. I have learned that "unanswered" prayer is evidence of "unfinished" preparation: someone or something is not quite ready for Him to intervene. Jesus is a *great* Healer, not an *impulse* Healer! He does all things WELL. He is never guilty of malpractice!

A few days later I was home. All functions were GO. My blood count was normal despite having been "bled out" and no transfusions. My brain function was essentially normal aside from the residual dizziness from the damaged inner ear. Soon my hair grew out from the sutured scalp, thicker than before. Above all, I was experiencing a new companionship with God.

Others who have had a trip to heaven report the same thing: Jesus is really real! Not just a God on high. Not a miracle-worker in Pilate's time, long gone. Not a super-mystical Judge on a throne scowling at earth's indiscretions. But instead, a living Person, a loving friend, a whispering Counselor, a compassionate Healer. A Man with nailholes from suffering for our sins. And a ready King in heavenly armor defending us from each poisoned arrow released from Hell. What a Savior!!!

CONTEMPLATION

"All scripture is given by inspiration of God and is profitable for doctrine, for reproof, for correction, for instruction in righteousness: so that the man of God may be thoroughly equipped for every good work."
2 Timothy 3:16, 17 (New Int'l. Version)

How slowly we learn! How little we listen! How painfully frequent are the battles between Christ and satan for our souls! Satan bruises us first before Jesus can heal us. Satan *never* asks permission of his victim; Jesus *always* does, then awaits our answers.

During the months of recovery I was impatient. Now I know I had much to learn. But then I complained. God had saved my soul as a child; now He had saved my life as an adult. But for what purpose? To burden my tiring wife? To worry my children? To add financial pressures at the office and home? Why not heal me all at once and let me return to my chosen work? Happily, God is able to handle peevish children—even old ones! My anguished prayers were always answered with a quiet Voice: "My grace is sufficient for thee."

And of course it was! We did not go broke. The worries were unfounded. My damaged nerve trunks, joints, and skull somehow performed well enough to satisfy the daily needs. The world kept turning. Up front God was being by Teacher; behind the scenes He was my

October, 1972.
Clearlake
"Doc" models his
Pomo headdress a few
weeks after his re-
turn from Paradise to
"God's Country" in
California.

Healer, expertly prescribing just enough grace, just enough power, and just enough faith to keep the Adversary off balance. Every time satan attacked, the "Two-edged Sword" drove him back!

My Healer is a specialist at dosages, I learned. It must shock Him, The Great Physician, to be repeatedly told by His untrained children just what to use and how much to dispense! Hardly ever do I hear a prayer, even from pulpits, which fails to include medical advice for the Savior's edification. Almost every request for financial, spiritual, or physical aid includes a recommendation as to *timing* and *dosage*. If there were no other proof of Jesus' sense of humor, it would be enough to note that occasionally He actually answers those prayers! With a loving smile He spoons out the requested amounts and then sits back to await the anxious prayers for antidotes. (Like a doting father, He knows that children grow up the hard way. Once He gives them free wills, they eagerly use them foolishly.)

Long ago He prepared the Universal Antidote for every misdeed: the Bible calls it Blood, His Blood, Jesus' Shed Blood! (Leviticus 17:11 starts the story of Heaven's blood bank ... it's a long story that stretches into Revelation.) It simply scares satan to death, because the Shed Blood instantly dissolves all the chains he has used to bind his victims whenever they call out His Name! I note that satan never possessed any blood of his own ... by nature he was a born loser from the beginning. Hallelujah! He can not *counterfeit* SHED BLOOD nor *counteract* it!

I was given some time to re-learn with childhood faith several childlike truths. Since Jesus Christ is Truth (God says so), then so is His Word. If God's Word says He "doeth all things well," then He doeth all things well—today. And since men do not know all truth (if any at all), then He does not need my advice when I pray: nor anybody's.

What He does need is our trust. I have found this not as easy to learn and confer as I would like! My natural five senses rebel, even recoil, at trusting what is not felt, smelt, seen, heard, or tasted. Jesus knows this: for 33 years He wore a mortal body so He could be tempted, afflicted, and hurt ... in all ways like as we are. He walked in my shoes before I did. He suffered for me before I did. He loved me and died before I did. Why? So he could arrange my healing before I even needed it! And He decided on the dosage and timing so I could best employ and enjoy it. And now He was teaching me the next lesson, step by step ... how to receive it. (My

Teacher must be smiling wearily as my schooling progresses so slowly!)

Could He teach me patience? Possibly not. But He could teach me its source. Long ago He had moved his Old Testament writers to give me some answers: "For whatsoever things were written *aforetime* were written for our learning, that we through *patience and comfort* of the Scriptures might have hope" (Romans 15:4). Again, "*In the past* God spoke to our ancestors many times in many ways through the prophets, but in these last days He has spoken to us through His Son" (Hebrews 1:1, 2).

These verses were telling me that before patience must come learning, and learning comes through searching the Word, "whatsoever things are written." Then He made it increasingly apparent that *Trust* must precede reading and patience! To read with closed eyes and mind is spiritually futile. Now I understood why Patience develops only as Trust grows. I must learn first from His Word for what to trust Him! Can I trust Him to handle indigestion? Heart trouble? Boils? Hemorrhoids? Infertility? Cancer? Hemorrhage? Blindness? Leprosy? Nervousness? Demon possession? Unbelief?

Jesus says so. On every page of scripture He records the proofs. He honors the *trust* of any "whosoever's" that call on Him—whether kings, kids, or princes or paupers! He obviously has a cure and comfort for every disease in my medical dictionary, even including death and sin which we doctors can not handle.

His Rx Blanks prescribe "Faith and Trust" which unbelievers read as "Foolishness" (see I Cor. 2:14 for proof). Dr. Jesus uses a variety of "ridiculous" therapies with amazing results: to wit,

Rx Anoint with oil	James 5:14
Rx Lay on hands	Matthew 8:15; 9:25, 29
Rx Fast and pray	Matthew 17:21
Rx Exercise faith	Matthew 9:22
Rx Intercede in prayer	James 5:15
Rx Touch a hem or cloth	Matthew 9:21
Rx Mud on the eyes & tongue	Mark 8:23; John 9:6
Rx Spit on the tongue	Mark 7:33
Rx Bind Satan	Matthew 18:18
Rx Duck under water 7 times	II Kings 5:14
Rx Cast out demons	Mark 5:8
Rx Agree together, 2 or more	Matthew 18:19

Throughout the Scriptures our Great Physician has had His writers sign the prescriptions "Thus Saith The Lord." When He was talking directly with His patients, He used His sovereign seal of "Verily, Verily, I Say. . . ." Either way, each time, His medicine worked miracles, then as now. In the healing arts, *He is AUTHORITY!*

Why? He *alone* holds the keys to the Library of Heaven where the many Books are stored—including His Anatomy Books! I want to share the excitement I experienced a while ago when He showed me Psalm 139— written for doctors who need to trust. I doubt that David fully realized what he was writing as the Lord guided his pen:

1. "Oh Lord, Thou hast (re)searched me and known me." (Imagine the excitement of seeing His research papers someday!)

2a. "Thou knowest my downsitting and my uprising." (He designs the musculo-skeletal apparatus.)

2b. "Thou understandeth my thoughts afar off." (God interprets and receives our projected thought waves.)

3. "Thou compasseth my path and my laying down."
    (He measures out our daily energy and our fatigue.)

4. "There is not a word in my tongue but Thou knowest it."
    (He has programmed our speech center and monitored it.)

13a. "For Thou hast possessed my reins."
    (He controls the delicate kidney functions for us.)

13b. "Thou hast covered me in my mother's womb."
    (He protects the embryo within fluids and membranes.)

14. "I am fearfully and wonderfully made."
    (My spirit and body are too complex for human understanding except for "awe and wonder.")

15. "My substance was not hid from thee when I was made in secret."
    (Genes, chromosomes, nuclei, molecules—all are open to God.)

16a. "Thine eyes did see my substance yet being imperfect."
    (God sees the 1-day embryo as a completed human while its cells are as yet undifferentiated! Note: Our Supreme Court can not identify it as human until the twentieth week!)

And then in the sixteenth verse David reveals an earth-shaking, argument-settling bit of medical news . . .

"And in Thy book all my members were written which in continuance (sequentially) were fashioned when as yet there was none of them."

In no uncertain language the Creator Himself herein reveals His Genesis modus operandi! BEFORE the "dust of the earth" was sculptured into an Adam, the great Anatomy Book had been written. BEFORE a single cell or organ was created, Jesus had set down the requisites for its form and function! Like the Great Architect who plans ahead, the Great Physician left no room for error, no room for satanic argument. His Adam would be perfect—in fact made after God's image—the supreme honor He could confer! Not by chance, not by evolution, BUT BY MY WORD, saith the Lord! This Adam (with his descendants) was to be His earthly TEMPLE.

Is it therefore any wonder that He loves *His* special handiwork? His very special accomplishment? Is it any wonder that He bore stripes to repair those special bodies; that He shed blood to buy them back after their owners had given them away? Is it any wonder that He alone knows how to equip a Human Repair Kit for use on house calls to His damaged Temples?

Should it surprise us that He keeps *special promises* locked in His Doctor's bag for use when requested?

When we trust Him, He unlocks His bag, and there on top we can clearly see two of these beautiful promises: signed "With love":

Rx "God shall supply ALL your need according to His riches in Christ Jesus." Philippians 4:19

Rx "I WILL come and heal him." Matthew 8:7

MIRACLE 34
Tell Them, Tell Them, Tell Them

"He brought me also up out of the horrible pit, out of the miry clay; and set my feet upon a rock, and established my goings." Psalm 40:2

For Maybelle and me it was a miracle just to be on this tour of Israel in April of 1977—our first tour anywhere after 40 years of phone calls, night calls, and house calls! Our lives had been enriched already by the TBN programs which Jan and Paul Crouch had broadcasted through the miracle ministry of Channel 40 TV from Mt. Wilson and Santa Ana. To millions they were already known as partners on "Praise the Lord" programs; to us they were friendly saints busied with the multiplying assignments hand-picked as His servants in these climactic times of the last days before His return.

Thursday our six buses inched down a steep hill and stopped off the narrow pavement. Scarcely had we left Jerusalem behind and here was Bethany already; and up the hill was Lazarus' tomb. We had been singing about "The Family of God" and "The Name of Jesus" and "How Great Thou Art," but I was totally unprepared for what Jesus had in store for me in that hillside! Off the buses we scrambled, each with his own thoughts as to what that day would bring.

April, 1977. TBN Israel Tour Bus No. 2. En route to Lazarus'
Tomb and to experience another miracle with Jesus as guide.

The guide had cautioned us that no one can know for
sure that this is the site to which Martha and Mary
summoned their friend Jesus to heal their sick brother. He
had been miles away across the Jordan (beyond the in-
tervening wasteland) to escape an angered mob bent on
stoning Him to death for doing miracles. He chose to delay
two extra days before the long trip back, in order to teach
Martha an *advanced lesson* in faith: as the Resurrection
and Life, He had no need to hurry, despite Martha's
pleading. She did not yet believe that her Jesus could
enliven dead cells just as readily as those dusty ones in the
original creation days. Nor did His doubting disciples!

The Scriptures described for me the events of that day on the sidehill: "Then Jesus said to them plainly, 'Lazarus is dead'. And I am glad for *your sakes* that I was not there (four days ago), to the intent that *you* may believe" (John 11:14, 15). Jesus wept then (not because of Lazarus' death but because of their unbelief). "Take ye away the stone," He continued as He looked into the hearts of the assembled throng: "Said I not unto you that if thou wouldst believe, thou shouldst see the GLORY OF GOD? . . . LAZARUS, come forth!" Then as He saw their hearts melting, He let them share the miracle: "Loose him and let him go." And the predicted result happened: "And many who had seen (the Glory of God) believed in Him." For us it seemed like only yesterday when Jesus had stood prayerfully on this hillside.

As we walked up the steep roadway to the low entrance I was marveling at those (three) miracles which had happened that day when Jesus lifted His eyes to His Father: dead cells restored, a bound body floated out of a tomb, and unbelief instantly cured! The mental picture was staggering. Then I thought what the *real* scene must have been for those bone-tired disciples hurrying from the Jordan and for those heart-sick relatives sobbing at the stone. And I could imagine the disappointed face of The Christ with His anguish over their little faith . . . and His heartbreak in knowing that His own tomb was awaiting Him only a fifteen furlongs and a few days away! Because of His Father's will He would voluntarily divest Himself of all divinity and power in order to be dead, wrapped, and raised three days later, in order to overcome death and to be declared by His loving Father as the only WORTHY LAMB in all creation! Then His face became radiant: "Father, I thank Thee that Thou hast heard me."

I ducked into the dark doorway and brushed away a tear to see better. The long narrow circling tunnel of stepping stones wound downward, lighted by six small dangling lamps. The two-storey descent to ground level took me through the centuries of debris from successive churches built over this shrine. A childsize doorway in the stone led to a burial room with a slab at one side. A single bulb hung from the ceiling. Only three persons at a time could crowd into this rocky eight-foot cubicle. When my turn came, I squeezed through the chiseled door-hole and stood up alongside two elderly ladies in an empty tomb . . . Just then the Lord blew the fuse! (All *my* life He had waited for this moment.)

The ladies screamed in the pitch blackness, and I reached out to re-assure them, "It's alright, ladies, the fuse simply blew. Let's be quiet till the guide replaces it."

Then the miracle started (perhaps the fourth in this tomb?)! To this day I can scarcely accept what happened; I can only share it . . . with a shudder. Suddenly the ladies were gone! There was total silence—not a rustle of clothing, not a sound of their frightened breathing, not even a whisper from the crowded staircase outside the tiny entrance. I had never known such total silence. Nor such blackness—like absolute blindness. Instantly I was experiencing total separation from everything, except . . .

In the twinkling of an eye Jesus was standing beside me! At the same moment the tomb was filled with heavenly light. (Jesus knew that without *His* light I could not see Him nor touch Him even if He were there: just as in our *daily* walk with Him we need not see nor touch His Spirit in order to know that He is *in* us!) As I looked into His Powerful Face with those piercing eyes of love, I heard again that Wonderful Voice that had spoken to me from the Shekinah cloud in my hospital room five years before:

"My son; I showed you heaven, now I show you hell. You must know about them both. In heaven I took away your fear; for two minutes now I give it back. You must be able to tell them they can choose heaven or hell, but *tell them* that I died to close hell and open heaven just for them. They must choose between My love and eternal life, or Satan's lies and eternal death. Tell them, tell them, tell them. There is yet a little time, but very little."

The voice was of One calling His sheep. Then He was gone, and my two minutes of hell started! Instantly I realized I was as a dead sinner being taken to the lowest bowels of the earth. The tomb became The Pit. A sense of absolute terror gripped my being. The immensity of my isolation in the stark darkness and soundless silence was overwhelming. I would have screamed but there was no voice.

If it were not for Jesus' explicit command that I tell about it, this experience would be too frightening to relate. I will never know whether that special tomb had ever been used by God to teach a lesson on Hell. Certainly as a sacred shrine in the Holy Word it must have been spared the desecration of housing a sinner's body under Satan's control. If so, I cherish this awful two-minute revelation all the more for God having used a hallowed tomb as a fitting contrast to the pit of Hades.

Praise the Lord for *only* two minutes of hell! Even so, it was too long. In the depths of earth my isolation was terrifying. No one could help but Jesus, and He was gone! My mind was lightning fast as it had been in heaven. Thoughts tumbled over one another: I would never see another person; I could not break out; I would never hear a voice again—either friend or enemy. Nothing to read. Nothing to look at. Nowhere to go. Even my own body-sounds were stilled in death. With terror came anger: hell-inspired curses flowed out in *silence*. My lips were silenced! Hate, wrath, cruelty, and insane rage rolled back and forth through me. Despite the utter silence I heard demons taunt me: Damn God! Damn people! Damn everything! Damn me! Especially damn Jesus for doing this to me when I hadn't done anything to Him—in fact I had always left Him totally alone! Damn Satan too, the dirty deceiver. He should burn for this! . . .

And then I noticed the *cold*. The kind that sickens and chills every cell just enough to ache but not get numb. There was no way ever to get warm, not in that dank pit! And the *smell*! Horrid, nasty, stale, fetid, rotten, evil . . . mixed together and concentrated. Somehow I knew instantly that these were the odors of my Pit-mates. Stinking, crawling, demons seen mentally delighting in making me wretched. The immensity of this depravity in which they were living and exulting was appalling. I would now have an eternity of inescapable nausea, besides all the rest of hell. My terror mounted until I was ready to collapse into utter hopelessness, crushing despair, abysmal loneliness. I was an eternally lost soul by my own choosing. I screamed but not a sound. The clammy wet walls held me crushed for eternity without escape, without a Savior, without anything to maintain sanity!

And then it was over. The lights flicked on. The two ladies squealed with delight. Voices were laughing on the outside stairway.

The guide peered through the small door and smiled: "This way, pah-leeze," and gestured to indicate that one can expect anything in his country.

I must have ascended the stone stairs because I was rejoined by my wife and party as we boarded bus number two. She told me that I was not "with it" the rest of that

happen"! Then a young or weak believer feels a sense of guilt over his supposed responsibility for the friend's illness, or for the friend's failure to be healed despite prayer. Satan's troops sit back and laugh with pride: they have shot down a potential witness for Jesus (Psalm 40:12-15)!

For the "hard-shelled" saint who has resisted the demon's oppressions so far, satan orders his crown of thorns! Now the fur starts to fly! This was the attack used on that greatest apostle of all, St. Paul. After satan had led the murderous mob to stone him to death at Lystra, and had failed to silence his praising lips when God had raised Paul from the dead outside the city gates, satan assigned his top strategist to the case! "Thorn-in-the-flesh" was his name, chief "buffeter" from the slime-line-up at Ft. PIT. If Paul could be silenced by pain, defeat, infirmities, reproaches, and distresses, certainly Colonel Thorn-in-the-flesh would do it! (Read the details in II Corinthians 12:1-12.)

This particular case was one of satan's greatest flops. Despite aching joints, failing eyes, jerking speech, bleeding stripes, clammy dungeons, lonesome cells, and deserting friends, Paul lifted hands and voice in continuous praise: "Most gladly (because His grace is sufficient for me) will I glory in my infirmities . . . reproaches, necessities, persecutions, for Christ's sake; for when I am weak, then am I strong!"

Unfortunately, many young or weak Christians cave in when Colonel Thorn attacks. As a physician, I see this spiritual collapse occurring in so many patients. I even get letters from a few "church people" lambasting me as a Christian doctor because my prescription failed to produce a cure; hence I have no right to claim that God can affect disease one way or another! "If your God is a

God of miracles (as I claimed) then why didn't one happen right there in the office, unless you are both phoneys?" (I can hear satan chuckling: "Now *that* is a *good* question, Doc; let's see you worm out of that one.")

Of course, satan's sneering query does not deserve any new answer. He already knows the scriptures, and can quote the answers. He merely hopes that we cannot withstand his arrows. Split-hoof can only defeat us when we falter! Satan knows that Christ told him personally: "Thou shalt not tempt the LORD" (Matthew 4:7)! He knows that Christ recognizes how the LIAR binds people with sickness even for years; and he is scared by any people who discover that Christ can "loose from bonds" (Luke 13:15-17). Satan knows the key to God's healing: viz, complete faith that He can do what He promises (James 5:14)! Satan also knows that Jesus cannot break a Divine Promise, including the one He made to all disciples: "If thou canst believe, all things are possible to him that believeth" (Mark 9:23).

Satan had clearly heard Christ drive home the point when He expelled the demon from the child with seizures: "If you have faith as a grain of mustard seed, you shall say unto this mountain (of demon-possession): 'Move from here to yonder place' (the PIT?), and it shall move; and NOTHING shall be impossible to you" (Matthew 17:20). Satan has read the final chapter wherein the BORN-LOSER loses! He and his ilk are cast into lasting fire (Revelation 20:7-10)!

His defeat leads to God's greatest miracle of love: the believer's right to victory over Satan—past, present, and future! Also—

The right to God's promises (unalterable)
The right to God's Love (immeasurable)
The right to God's riches (unsearchable)
The right to Eternal Life (irrevocable)
The right to instant communication (prayer)
The right to His Spirit (infallible Comforter)

Each "right" belongs to the believer because it has been prepared as a personal gift to him by God the Father in return for merely accepting the gift of His Son. What a miracle (John 1:12, 13)!

DO YOU WANT THAT MIRACLE RIGHT NOW? YOU DO? HONESTLY?

Alright then! Do this: bend your knee, raise you hand, open your heart, and say out loud:

> "Lord, I thank you for forgiving my sins. I now believe You. I accept Your love for me. And I love You too! Be my Lord and Savior right now! Amen."

Now, go and tell the world about YOUR miracle! And praise the LORD!

> "He who testifieth these things saith, SURELY I come quickly. Amen. Even so, Come, Lord Jesus" (Revelation 22:20).

~ Citation ~

FOR THE AWARD OF THE HONORARY DEGREE DOCTOR OF EDUCATION TO DR. RICHARD E. EBY

Richard Engle Eby, D.O., D.Sc., F.A.C.O.O.G., was born in Massachusetts on June 26, 1912. Dr. Eby received his education at Pittsfield, Massachusetts High School, Wheaton College and the College of Osteopathic Physicians and Surgeons in Los Angeles, California. In 1964, the Kansas City College of Osteopathy and Surgery conferred the Honorary Degree of Doctor of Science. Following his graduation from the College of Osteopathic Physicians and Surgeons, he interned at Los Angeles County Hospital and took residency training there. Subsequently, he became Chairman of the Department of Obstetrics at the College of Osteopathic Physicians and Surgeons in California. He was president of the Kansas City College of Osteopathy and Surgery from 1963 to 1965. Later he served as Chairman of the Department of Obstetrics and Gynecology at KCOM.

Dr. Eby has been an active member and Fellow of the American College of Osteopathic Obstetricians and Gynecologists and served as president of the group from 1956 to 1957. He has held the posts of Assistant Executive Director of the American Osteopathic Association and Trustee of the American Osteopathic Association. He has been elected to the presidencies of the Osteopathic Physicians and Surgeons of California, and the California Osteopathic Hospital Association. To enumerate his many other professional accomplishments would require more time than is available today. At present, Dr. Eby is in private practice in Pomona, California. He was co-founder and Chairman of the Board of Trustees of the Park Avenue Hospital, Pomona, California and currently serves as Chairman of Obstetrics and Gynecology there. He has been an active member of Kiwanis, the American Association of Advancement of Science and numerous churches and musical organizations.

Dr. Eby is an accomplished musician and numbers fishing among his hobbies. Dr. and Mrs. Eby are the parents of two children, Walter and Carol.

In February, 1971, the journal Maternal and Child Health awarded Dr. Eby its Distinguished Physician Award. The journal citation contains the following, and I quote:

"Where ever he goes, and in all his varied endeavors, Dick Eby has made multitudes of friends. His keen interest in people, his ever ready smile, his spontaneous wit and his charm have endeared him to his patients, his friends, his family and his colleagues. These personal qualities, plus his magnificent achievements in professional life, have made him an unquestioned 'distinguished physician.'"

For the past three years, at considerable personal sacrifice, Dr. Eby has returned to the campus of the Kirksville College of Osteopathic Medicine to provide instruction to our third year students in obstetrics and gynecology. He is truly an outstanding educator, a brilliant scholar and a compassionate physician. The faculty has nominated and the Board of Trustees has unanimously voted that the Honorary Degree of Doctor of Education in Osteopathic Medicine be conferred upon Dr. Richard E. Eby.

May 22, 1972
Kirksville College of Osteopathic Medicine
Kirksville, Missouri 63501